LANDSCAPE INTO LITERATURE

LANDSCAPE

INTO

LITERATURE

A Writers' Anthology

Edited by Kay Dunbar

Green Books
in association with

WAYS WITH WORDS

First published in 2005
by Green Books Ltd
Foxhole, Dartington
Totnes, Devon TQ9 6EB
www.greenbooks.co.uk

in association with

Ways With Words
Droridge Farm,
Dartington,
Totnes, Devon TQ9 6JG
www.wayswithwords.co.uk

Cover design by Stephen Bristow
Photos © Stephen Bristow
Illustration © Clifford Harper

Text printed by MPG Books Ltd, Bodmin, Cornwall
on Five Seasons Stone-White 100% recycled paper

British Library Cataloguing in Publication Data
available on request

ISBN 1 903998 55 7

Contents

Introduction

Kay Dunbar

For fourteen years I have organised the Ways With Words Literature Festivals. These take place in landscapes that have inspired writers in the past and continue to do so today—Cumbria, Devon and Suffolk. The running of the festivals takes place from a green oak barn in the middle of fields: ours is probably the only festival whose address is a farm, though Droridge Farm is not a working farm any more. Well, it is a working farm, but as Seamus Heaney would say, we dig with our pens, not our spades. Once our barn would have hummed with cattle lowing, chickens clucking; now it is filled with the chorus of phones ringing, computers cackling. I won't stretch the comparison with talk of fieldmice replaced with Apple Mac mice.

The land around us is still farmed. The field next to our office ("one oak field", as we call it, for obvious reasons) is ploughed, tilled and planted with rotating crops. Another field is filled with Jersey calves in the summer; this winter sheep replaced them. Cabbages, cows, lambs, oak trees, blackberries: none of these has much to do with literature festivals, yet for me they mark the rhythm of our working life as much as the recurring pattern of the year's festivals. They are also a source of inspiration and relaxation. Many ideas are hatched (to use a farming metaphor), while staring over the top of my computer to the tangle of ivy on an old stone wall. I can't resist beginning emails to a publisher in London, "Greetings from a misty (damp, wet, windy, and, less often, sunny) Devon," because the weather here can't be ignored as it can in towns. Sometimes when I am on the phone to a writer I interrupt our conversation with, "Oh, a pheasant has just walked by." These snapshots of Devon are offerings from the countryside to the city, the soil to the paving stones. The land, the weather, the wildlife and the sky inextricably interact with selling tickets, producing programmes; all the daily business of putting on literature festivals. And increasingly it is very busy; there are always deadlines to meet. Better communications mean more communication, and we often seem to be chasing our tails— to use another metaphor from the natural world. But the busier we are, the more I need to stop and observe the countryside around us, to see what the farmer has planted in one oak field, to go into the orchard and pick up the apples, to rake up the leaves. When we go away, the list of jobs for the office staff to do includes feeding the doves, watering the rocket seedlings and picking courgettes. Land and literature are closely linked in the preparation of our literature festivals.

Over the time that I have run Ways With Words, I have heard hundreds of writers talk at our festivals about how they write, where they write, where inspiration comes from. Frequently I have noticed that whatever a writer's subject, landscape often features in the process or the product. Childhood environments, the natural world, place and memory are all part of the rich compost of prose and poetry.

Many biographers have been to the festival. Wordsworth, Coleridge, Laurie Lee, Virginia Woolf, Charles and Emma Darwin, Vera Brittain, Derek Jarman, Augustus John, Iris Murdoch, Eric Gill, D. H. Lawrence, Matisse and so many others have had their life stories told by their biographers at Ways With Words. Most of these have said that they need to explore the personal landscapes of their subjects. Without knowing the places that have mattered to them, they can't form a complete picture of their biographees. Many literally follow in their subjects' footsteps: travelling the same path as Wordsworth through the

Duddon Valley, walking in the lush greenness of Laurie Lee's Slad, picnicking amongst the bluebells of John Mortimer's Thames Valley, standing on the shingle at Dungeness in Derek Jarman's garden. Andrew Motion told of how he sailed a small boat from the River Thames to Rome, to follow Keats' last journey. Richard Holmes wrote a book called *Footsteps* in which he tells of how he repeated Coleridge's journeys while writing the poet's biography. The title of his book has become a verb, and fellow biographers talk of going 'footstepping'.

Thousands of poems have been read at our festivals, many of which have been about landscape. Alice Oswald has read about the River Dart, which runs by our festival site in Devon. Jacob Polley has read poems with Cumbrian settings at our festival by Derwentwater. Simon Armitage writes poems about his native Yorkshire.

At our festival by the North Sea in Southwold, Roger Deakin told of swimming in that wild, grey sea on Christmas day, an incident he writes about in his book *Waterlog*: "breakers the colour of dirty knickers licking up the beach". When he came to our literature festival in Cumbria one March, he led a delegation of writers up the mountain to swim in a very cold, black tarn.

This rich fermentation between landscape and literature gave me the idea for this book, so I asked writers to analyse how the alchemy worked for them. A frequent theme running through the essays is the inescapable influence of childhood experiences. Some give a slice of autobiography: "It's the beginning of the 1950s ... I'm reading a comic, when suddenly a butterfly lands on my shoe," Brian Patten writes.

Rain falling on a tin bath held over the head; walking over frozen bogs on Dartmoor; fishing for minnows, bullheads and tommy-whiskers on the Pennine fells; sailing through whirlpools of phosphorescence at night: these early experiences of the natural world transmute into literature when childhood moves into adulthood.

Several writers claim that writing a book happens partly indoors and partly outdoors. Richard Mabey quotes the Latin phrase *solvitur ambulando*—you can sort it out by walking. Other writers sort it out by contact with the elements in different ways: gardening, cycling, swimming, sailing.

Novelists, true to form, mix fact and fiction with breathtaking abandon. "In 1993 I killed a woman . . . She died . . . on the Mull of Kintyre," is James Long's startling beginning.

Hunter Davies, who spends six months of his year in the Lake District, started his piece: "I don't like writing about landscape." It was an unexpected, slightly shocking admission, but there are many surprises when several different writers respond to the same topic. It is the mix of styles, experiences and opinions that makes the highly personal writing in this book moving, informative and entertaining— usually all at once.

Kay Dunbar
Festival Director
Ways With Words
Droridge Farm
Dartington
Devon

Early Influences

Trainspottering

Roger Deakin

Roger Deakin's account of his swimming journey
through Britain, *Waterlog*, captured the imagination
of many readers. At present he is working on a book
on woods. He lives in Suffolk where he swims in his
moat, the rivers and the sea.

IN THE DAYS BEFORE they pruned its last syllable along with the branch lines, my father worked for British Railways, and we were always travelling on the cheap or free tickets that went with the job. Rather grandly, they called them 'Privilege Tickets'. In a modern sense, we were model citizens: we had no family car, and travelled only on foot, bike, bus or train. At weekends we went walking in the Chilterns equipped with butterfly net, binoculars, a Sauternes-bottle minnow trap, saucepans for blackberries or rosehips, and my News Chronicle I-Spy books. On holidays we went much further, to Cornwall, Scotland, France, Italy, always by train, because even on the Continent our travel was subsidised. As an only child, I spent more time than most boys in the trance of the train's rhythm, gazing out of railway carriage windows at glimpses of other lives. Auden catalogued a selection of them in 'Night Mail'. I remember women hanging out washing in Welwyn Garden City, men on allotments, bargees on the Grand Union Canal, train-spotters at Crewe, hens spilling out of their arks in fields outside the Ovaltine factory on the way to Coventry. Such glimpses tantalised me: I began to imagine these lives and places for myself.

My father's side of the family were all railway people, and in an era of steam engines, the romance of the railways easily equalled, to us, the romance of the Navy. Steam locomotives were organic, crafted, living, coughing, panting things. Railwaymen were fiercely loyal to their trade and tribe, and I was aware of the strong camaraderie that existed between them wherever we went. They proudly tended beautiful station gardens and were sometimes heroes, too, as in Charles Parker and Ewan McColl's famous radio ballad, The Ballad of John Axon, about the engine driver who died saving his train. Occasionally, as my father's son, I would even get an unofficial ride on the footplate of an engine on a quiet branch line, be lifted up to reach the handle, and sound the whistle. I never collected mere abstract train numbers, but loved the power, the plumbed beauty of the steam locomotives, and would run with my playmates to the end of our street in the evenings to watch the *Flying Scotsman* go by, beginning its night journey to Glasgow. This time my glimpse of another world was from the outside in: waiters laying the tables for dinner, lights in the portholes of the mail coach, with its lacrosse-stick contraption to catch the mail bags hung out on gibbets along the line, passengers glancing absently out at us as we stood waving.

Later, when I first saw the opening scene of Satyajit Ray's *Pather Panchali*, I felt a jolt of recognition as the young Apu raced through the fields of maize outside his village, following his older sister, in time to see the train go by. It is his first hint of an outside world existing beyond his rural village. I still live within hearing of a railway today: the line from Norwich to London at the far side of my furthest meadow. I can wade through the hay in summer and, just like Apu, see trains on their way to other worlds, remembering how they gave me the freedom and impetus to travel, to explore, to daydream, read and write.

A train journey still sets my imagination going. All my early adventures were by train. All through my teens I used to travel alone through France on the *Golden Arrow* and the *Train Bleu* to stay with my pen-friend Jean-François in Menton. Waking up early in a *wagon lit* to the Mediterranean dawn on the bright sea towards Toulon, trundling past a flat calm beyond the sand dunes of Frejus, and a first sighting of octopus fishermen clambering about the rocks of Cap Martin with their long canes and olive-leaf lures: such moments remain vividly imprinted in me. Jean-Francois was a railway child like me and enjoyed the same travel concessions, so we tripped back and forth across the Channel as casually as a pair of diplomats, and I have the railways to thank for a whole second language.

The first thing I do on arrival in any foreign city is to go straight to the railway station and gaze at the destination boards. In Moscow you can walk along platforms that seem a mile long and see families preparing samovars in the dimly-lit sleeping compartments of trains bound for Omsk, Odessa, Archangel, Astrakhan or Almaty. From Almaty you can journey, as Fitzroy

Maclean once did, 500 miles by slow train to Tashkent, and from Tashkent to Samarkand. In fact, all the most memorable journeys I've made in recent years have been long and relatively slow.

Setting out on a train journey, like reading a novel, does something interesting to time. Once on a train, you cannot be in a hurry, and your sphere of activity is strictly, relaxingly, limited. Beginning a long journey, from Prague, say, skirting the Tatra Mountains via Slovakia into Ukraine as far as Lviv, you resign yourself to travelling all night and all the next day. But the resignation gains you a kind of freedom: access to another dimension of time. In his novel *If on a winter's night a traveller*, Italo Calvino considers the contradiction of writing long novels today: "The dimension of time has been shattered, we cannot love or think except in fragments of time each of which goes off along its own trajectory and immediately disappears. We can rediscover the continuity of time only in the novels of that period when time no longer seemed stopped and did not yet seem to have exploded, a period that lasted no more than a hundred years."

Perhaps on some trains, too, we can "rediscover the continuity of time". On trains more or less anywhere in the old Soviet empire, for example, time still feels measured with a pendulum. When you cross the border into Ukraine at the reassuring-sounding Tchop, you have a leisurely two hours to kill while your carriage is hoisted into mid-air and the bogeys changed to a different gauge. Winding past logging camps or crossing high bridges over swollen mountain rivers, the train climbs at a deliberate enough pace for you to take a good look inside every geranium-filled signalbox, whose occupants all stand to attention in the open doorways, holding small flags aloft as you pass. In Ukraine, at least, they still take their railways seriously. In Rumania, a friend and I once took all day over lunch in a train that snaked very gently through orchards in the Carpathian hills from Bucharest to Cluj. The tablecloths were collages of many a past sitting, but a compensating vase of fresh wild flowers graced every table and the waiters kept the Georgian champagne flowing as Transylvania unfolded before us and our lunch cooked slowly on a coal range.

Night trains give you the most measured sense of time because you inhabit your compartment that much more intimately, lulled into sleep by the rhythmic tattoo of wheels and rail-joints or the steady screech of steel on steel as you follow the contours of hillsides. Thus you experience two layers of dreams, waking to the moving pictures crossing the window at twenty-eight frames per minute, telegraph wires rising and swooping like a scratch on the negative. Assuming you are sensible enough not to carry the umbilical mobile, you are blissfully insulated from distraction.

There was a time when every rural or seaside railway sidings had a camping coach or two retired from active service to rest against the buffers as holiday lodgings. A row of Pullman coaches still stands silhouetted against the sea looking out to St Michael's Mount at Marazion. You pass them in the train shortly before Penzance on the way to the Scillies. They are shamefully derelict now, abandoned national treasures, casualties of the tragic fragmentation of our railways. But they were once camping coaches, giving working families a taste of Pullman luxury like a week in a stately home.

I have a version of a camping coach out in a meadow, tucked in a hedge. It is an old wooden goods wagon, a cattle truck, sturdily built with an oak and steel frame, double-boarded in pitch pine, with a sliding door, wooden steps, an iron Tortoise stove, and a stainless-steel chimney-pipe with a chinaman's hat. At either end, you slide a piece of plywood up to open a small window, and the whitewashed ceiling is bowed on barrelled rafters of oak. This is where I often work and sleep as soon as the spring comes, part-train, part-den. Like the shepherd's hut in the next meadow, it arrived here in a bad way and required as careful repair as a boat.

Working in the railway wagon with the door wide open to the south is a way of being both inside and out, alive to the great glory of Suffolk: the weather. We have no mountains to hide the magnificence of the clouds, but on some days they *are* our mountains. The open door is my railway carriage window and the changing weather is like changing scenery. I love the stillness of dawn, the honking of geese going over to the fens along the River Waveney at dusk, or the barking of foxes at night. When the wind gets up and beats the roof with the overhanging maple-boughs, or lashes the wagon with rain, I light the stove for company and a cat may steal in and curl up too.

My cultivation of a shed or two like this, sequestered from the house, is not unusual. Most people like a den, and it often represents a return to some sense in earlier life of independence and security: of a more animal existence. While the trains and the rambling gave me a keen appreciation of geography, I know that the cabin my father built at the end of the garden for me and various animal friends shaped my imagination quite as strongly by giving me a taste for the pleasures of staying put. I didn't know it at the time, but he was much influenced by Thoreau and had his own part-time retreat: a shed complete with nine bean-rows in the bee-loud glade of the local allotments. My place, a wooden shanty that soon sprouted rabbit and guinea-pig hutches, more than one vivarium and a pigeon-loft, was just as much of a refuge from the trials of family life and school for me. I spent hours up there communing with various creatures and was allowed a camp-bed to sleep out in the summer. I remember the toasty aroma of the animals' straw bedding, fresh hay, the rank hogweed I collected each morning, and the sound of the multiplying rodents all chewing contentedly. My parents had the good sense to leave me and my chums alone in the cabin and in the various outlying dens we built in the local spinney.

Later on, I was allowed to use the workshop, and was given a carpentry set. Between workshop and cabin, I was learning the noble art of pottering, the beginning of all invention. Like walking, it is a form of meditation and invariably throws up ideas. I do my pottering in the vegetable garden, in the workshop, along the hedgerows or round the woodshed.

I go swimming in my moat, walk into the woods, ride my bike along the lanes, turn the compost, put up some shelves. I have stayed put in the same house for more than half my life now. But I still love to go off exploring from time to time, or hide out in a cabin to read or write. Having a fixed centre, I feel easier in my freewheeling as I did on those early train journeys. I can't imagine writing without travelling, or without staying put either: questing and pottering both seem to suit me. One day, if I keep working at it, I'll be a master-potterer.

Rooted in One Dear Perpetual Place

Kathleen Jones

Kathleen Jones' poetry, fiction and biographies have won several awards. Amongst her biographies are *A Passionate Sisterhood, The Lives of the Sisters, Wives and Daughters of the Lake Poets,* and *Catherine Cookson: the biography.* She is currently working on a novel, and on the biography of Katherine Mansfield.

ATTITUDES TO THE ENGLISH LAKE DISTRICT have always been ambivalent. The dramatic landscape with its icy torrents, which inspired Wordsworth and Coleridge, disgusted Charles Lamb, just as it repels modern visitors for whom a holiday is not complete without sunshine and a palm-fringed beach. Even residents have been heard to complain about the lack of comfort, warmth and good weather! But for me the mountains and lakes are essential to my psyche, and I never cease to be moved by the fluctuations in the weather—the patternings of cloud and light that Southey observed "might almost make a painter burn his brushes, as the sorcerers did their books of magic". I belong to this landscape in some mysterious, primaeval way, rooted in its contradictions.

I spent the early years of my childhood on a remote croft, miles up an unsurfaced track, high up in the Cumbrian fells. The front and back doors opened straight out onto the hillside, and cows and horses were stabled next to the living accommodation. There was no electricity or telephone; water came from a spring on the hillside, and the only toilet was an earth closet. The latter was not regarded as a green amenity in the fifties and sixties—more a social embarrassment. Nor was the spring environmentally innocent: the body parts of unfortunate frogs were liable to appear through the tap at certain times of the year, and after the Sellafield 'accident' which dusted the hills with radioactivity and caused my father to pour buckets of milk down the drain for weeks on end, it was invisibly contaminated. But we still drank the water—there was no alternative.

My parents were 'off-comers': my mother a land girl displaced by the war; my father the child of an Irish immigrant family, cattle drovers and small farmers, displaced by poverty. He loved the land, loved farming, but could not afford to buy his own farm. So he laboured for another landowner in return for the croft. The people who wrenched a living from the land around us belonged to that land as we could not. They could all trace their ancestry back a thousand years to the Vikings who had settled there. Our neighbours never used their surnames but were known by their holdings: Willy the Crewe, Bobby the Row, Maggie the Inskip. The landscape was named in Norse: a river valley was a Wath or a Syke, streams were Becks, and the small strip of tree shelter behind the house was a Garth. The dialect spoken by everyone looked towards Oslo rather than London. It was a strong language, with few passive verbs or feminine word endings: if you were busy you were 'thrang', talk was 'crack'. It was muscular on the tongue and picturesque on the ear. The Queen's English spoken at home or at school seemed colourless by comparison.

Most people over fifty had never been further than the nearest small town in their entire lives, and few of them could read or write more than their names. Having no electricity, there was no television to fill the evenings. People walked to each other's houses and had 'good crack'. As they talked, they peopled the landscape around me with stories: Old Sworley who had hanged himself in the barn believing that he had killed his wife by pitching her down the well (in fact she'd managed to climb out and run off to Carlisle); the woman whose ghost was supposed to walk the track on winter nights, where her children had been lost in a snowstorm; how people had burned their furniture to keep warm through the winter of '47; how Billy the Hope had spent three days floundering through the snow with a horse and sled to fetch the supplies for his starving family. His story, as they told it, was a tale worthy of a Greek epic.

And on those fireside nights I learned my own family stories, as I listened to my father and grandfather talking about ancestors who went across the sea on sailing ships to bring back cargos of bananas and marry exotic women; of others who drove herds of cattle from Ireland to London; or despaired over errant children, disinherited their offspring and fought bitterly over religion. These were stories they had learned from their own grandparents. I was aware, even at nine or ten, that I was listening to an unbroken memory line going back two hundred years— stories passing like heirlooms from one generation to another. The tellers seemed to know exactly what great-great-grandmother Bridie had said to her daughter Frances Theresa when she came home with a baby she wasn't supposed to have, fathered by a footman at the house where she was in service. The fine rooms, the uniforms, the very porcelain crockery she washed in a lead-lined sink were all there in the story, leaping like a hologram in the firelight before my eyes. The account of my great-great-uncle Edward who had stood preaching the gospel of temperance outside his father's pub on a Tyneside quay, was pure Catherine Cookson. It was hardly surprising that I grew up with a love of history, language and narrative that was somehow equated with the wild, untamed landscape beyond the kitchen door.

My parents were both book lovers. My mother could recite huge chunks of Shakespeare, Milton and Wordsworth. My father was more of a Marcus Aurelius man, and very fond of the King James bible. Every three weeks the library van would arrive at a road junction one and a half miles away, and my mother and I would trek down to it to collect the maximum allowance of books—which, as a fast reader, had to be made to last the full three weeks. It wasn't long before the reading became writing, and by the time I was eight or nine I was composing poems and stories of my own. I spent my senior school years writing for teenage magazines—witty pieces about trying to be a trendy teenager in Wellingtons, or the dangers of milking cows in stiletto heels. Like many a budding Lakeland author, I had to escape the influence of all the other writers who had become associated with the landscape—particularly William Wordsworth. The answer seemed to be to leave. I was sixteen, restless, my head full of poetry and the thirst for new experiences. I left for London, swearing never to return until I'd achieved my ambitions. I wanted to go and live in the real world, rather than a rural backwater where life was a hundred years behind the times, to go to discos and have proper plumbing. Above all, I wanted to be a writer.

But in London I was lost. Naïve, hopelessly unsophisticated, I hated city life. It was arid and claustrophobic. I hated the cramped bedsit with its unending view of more bedsit windows, the crowded tubes, the tedious clerical job, concrete horizons, grimed with soot and human detritus and more people than I could ever have imagined in one place at one time. I felt stifled, lonely and afraid, but was too proud to go home. Far from inspiring me to write, I dried up altogether.

An impulsive teenage marriage was followed by ten years following my husband around Africa and the Middle East. My primitive childhood proved to be good training for life in undeveloped countries. Exile sharpened feelings and memories, and I began to write about home—not England, but Cumbria. One of my first broadcast pieces for the Qatar Broadcasting Corporation was about life on a Cumbrian hill farm from the point of view of an expatriate wife. I knew then, as soon as the words took shape, that I would have to go back. A few more years spent in an English city, first as a wife and then as a single parent only confirmed that knowledge. I took a university degree, living in a cramped rooftop flat with four children all at different educational stages, fantasising about space and solitude. I began to dream about the Lake District and woke one morning crying to realise that I was still in my city flat.

The first two biographies were written in that crowded, noisy flat while the children were at school, or late at night when they were all in bed. I also began to write poetry which found an audience and a publisher, writing about what I cared most deeply about—the landscape of my childhood and the people who inhabited it. Not the romantic landscape of tourist postcards, but the reality of scratching a living on marginal land, where severe weather can wipe out a flock of sheep in a few hours and make the difference between survival and bankruptcy. Then in 1991 I was finally able to return home. At first I was treated as an off-comer, because I had lost my accent and become a stranger. But being there, re-connecting with the person I had been as a child, was very important for me. For the first time in my life I ceased to feel like a displaced person and felt whole. And it had other consequences.

One day, researching a short piece for a school's programme, I discovered in the Dove Cottage library, manuscripts of journals and letters written by the women of the Wordsworth and Coleridge families. I remembered how, as a teenager, I had been offered the option of boarding at Keswick Grammar School in order to avoid the long journey to and from school during the week, and had visited the dormitory, housed in Greta Hall, where Coleridge and Southey had lived with their families and which had hardly been altered since they left. The Wordsworth legend of Dove Cottage and the daffodils was also part of my childhood. Now I realised that William and Dorothy had like me been returning exiles, and that Southey and Coleridge were two of the original off-comers. To a young girl, Wordsworth had seemed something of an enigma: how had such poetry come from such a dry stick of a man? But Coleridge had always attracted me, with his reckless spirit, his enormous, visionary intellect—an idealist without a scrap of commonsense. Southey I knew little about. As I read through the archive boxes of unpublished material, I became fascinated by the lives of their respective wives, sisters and daughters, and the light their journals and letters cast on the characters of the men they lived with.

I decided to write the story of the 'Lake Poets' from the women's point of view. My own childhood—familiarity with unheated stone houses and the peculiarities of black kitchen ranges, isolation and the problems of transport in remote places—gave me a substantial insight into the privations they had had to endure. Their lives were very far from the Romantic legend of love and poetry in a cottage. There is nothing romantic about standing in a damp 'back' kitchen on cold flagstones with an icy gale blowing under the door, putting wet sheets through a gigantic mangle with hands raw from the combination of water and cold and the abrasive surfaces of heavy linen bedclothes. I decided to write it as a story, rather than an academic history, and *The Passionate Sisterhood* became my most successful book, but it would never have been written if I hadn't returned to live in the Lake District.

I go back regularly to the farm where I was brought up. My father's ashes are scattered there; his grit lodging stubbornly among the tufts of feral grass he spent a lifetime trying to tame. My mother, true to the tradition of ambivalence, remembers the flagstones and the mangle with a shudder and has requested a more comfortable resting place. I will probably follow my father and ask to have my dust returned to the hills where I was born and brought up, and where I feel part of an ongoing narrative about people and their place in the landscape.

Beyond the Rope's End:
Exploring the far side of landscape, through poetry
Alan Peacock

Alan Peacock was born and brought up in the Pennines, and has been based in Devon since 1988. In between, he has lived and worked in Scotland, East Africa and Northern Ireland, where he began publishing poetry. He has produced four books of poetry and a volume of *Collected Poems* (Hawthorn Press, 2003), from which all the poems in this chapter are taken. He works in environmental education. Walking the South West coastal path has inspired some of his recent poetry.

A GREY AFTERNOON, mid-December 1960; I am travelling home from University for the first time, on the coach from Manchester to Burnley. Take this journey with me ...

We are dawdling through urban industrial sprawl, along the valleys of buried rivers, Irwell and Roch, until we start to climb steeply up the Rossendale Fells, by Crawshawbooth, Loveclough and Dunnockshaw. Distant points of light are coming on as we pass Clowbridge reservoir on the treeless, peaty moor top. We begin to descend; the windscreen widens to cinemascope, a big view opens up ahead. I know the names of every outcrop and whaleback; Boulsworth, Pinhaw, Sharphaw, Pendle, Catlow, Longridge and in the faint distance, Pen-y-ghent and Ingleborough. But what fixes this journey in my mind are not these Nordic names but the slate-greys, reds, purples, blacks, silvers; an unforgiving Turner-esque sunset-scape.

Not for years did this revelation find its words. I had paradoxical, conflicting feelings on seeing this *as* landscape, for the first time; brutal, cold, painful, dark, yet beautiful. Here is the poem that finally emerged.

> Slit between moor and cloud is a watering eye
> of sky, rubbed bloodshot at the edge of dark
> by cold thumbs of wind; its pain
> clenches the skinned, arthritic knuckles, stiff
> and bitten since teeth of ice
> tore away all hopes of sun.
> You scan this crumbled flesh; catch
> a stale stink in the pitted joints; feel
> the immense majority of death
> and call it beautiful.

As a child, these same fells had been no more than the horizon that bound my world of mills, canals, becks, cow pasture, drumlins, hedges. We walked, birds'-nested, made dens, cycled, jumped becks; fished for minnows, bullheads and tommywhiskers. We went far afield, by current standards; but always felt close to home. Not until my twenties did I begin to explore the high fells. So come with me again, and look more closely ...

The Pennine fells are gritstone and limestone, shale and slate, scars and tarns, potholes and sinks, lead-mines, flues, leats, bields, laithes and sheep. They are defined by the dry-stone walls, built to keep people and stock off the fells. Strangely, we have no poet of the Pennine enclosures; John Clare never came north. He would not have liked what he saw.

Walls

They lope down fellsides at half light,
tired miners from worked-out seams,
as derelict as the shattered flues
where moss drips in the dark.

On the tops, they act as landmarks in mist
and blunt the wind, which sings cold
through holes where rubble has settled.
The capstones shift, as if to shatter.

No longer barriers to sheep, that wander
like old ladies picking bilberries,
their cavities become black nests
in which warm droppings are laid.

Pecked from the ground a pick's throw away,
heaped in tattoos on the moor's back
when bog and bracken became someone's land,
each winter's heaving frost crumbles

the rough grit back to pebbly silt;
to be carried down at glacier pace
and found in insignificant fragments—
relics of miners, the last mammoth.

My landscape, then, was to do with limestone, gritstone, water and sky; and I learned that stone was more than the geologist, artist or mountaineer saw. It was not until I travelled, however, that I came to learn the many languages of stone; the ankle-breaking granite of Penwith, the basalt organ-pipes of the Antrim coast, the volcanic plug that is Arthur's Seat, the warm, red sandstone of south Devon. I began to explore this, in 'Stone Gods':

> "The behaviour of stone is time-dependent:
> under slow, constant pressure, it bends—"
> (the TV geologist showed us,
> with a sheet of plastic)—
> "while under sudden pressure, it breaks".
> The plastic broke.
>
> I thought of all the stone I knew:
> gritstone edges creased by weathering winds,
> skulled and gargoyled limestone,
> pencils of basalt, granite annealed
> as tired volcanoes cooled.
> His gods were not the same as mine.

Stone shapes the landscape as much as hair, eye colour and skin shape our personalities. I 'found' the face of the next poem in a cliff near Zennor, on the granite 'toe' of England.

Penwith

> Pulse: lunar, normal.
> Blood pressure: zero, constant.
> One eye put out, the other
> focused on infinity.

Tongue, beard and brow
of the first beached Viking:
unkempt, scarred by the helmet's rim.
Smile of the world's last whale

in dying. Good
for another few million years.

But however stark these images seem, I now see them as the nearer, safer side of landscape. You can venture further, they tell me, as long as you keep hold of the rope. Here I am then, holding onto my rope, watching a river empty into the sea:

Exe

Here is our river at night;
black, unwarmed,
necklaced around with light.

A known face, blank now, and wide,
moved by deep flow
and wind, and eddy, and tide.

Most people have turned their backs
into car or pub,
familiar homeward tracks.

Our boat comes in on the swell;
the bow dips
and lifts, ready to tell

in stillness, what we have seen
and feared,
not knowing what it might mean.

We tie up in the current, and find
our reflection
to read by, with a mind

To kiss, reassure and warn.
Light holds to light.
We will be gone by dawn.

And here, I try making sense of one landscape in relation to another, whilst sitting for hours by a small tarn on the top of the fells between Littondale and Wharfedale.

Birks Tarn

Sit long enough
for the screeching small gulls
you thought you had disturbed
to settle back
on the warm peat;

sit long enough
to spot the black-backed gull
that sent them up
and would soon devour
their eggs.

Sit long enough
to take in the bulk
of well-built limestone,
the scoured forehead of Buckden Pike
and a dozen look-alike peaks.

Watch tarn-ripples diffract
between headlands of bare peat,
their minute swell
blast the sky's harebell blue
to the furthest fells.

Sit long enough in silence
to be honoured with the secrets
of larks, curlew, pipits, grouse,
the usual ravens.
A bee.

Sit long enough to be able to set
the skylark's tune
in counterpoint
to the minute swell
of this blue-mirror tarn.

And after all, sit long enough,
to rest your eyes and mind
on another ebb; on the warmth
of smooth sea-stones,
the breath of a retreating wave;

on Sanderling at the water's edge,
their winter wing-spots
flickering over the strand;
on Gannet and Shearwater,
wide-winged, unwilling to make land.

Landscape, then, was my term for wilderness seen from its margins, where I could look it in the eye, and retreat down my safety-rope with a collection of images, metaphors, feelings. It is only when I let go of the rope that the 'out there' ceases to be landscape, and becomes something much more intense and ultimately life-threatening. I rarely do this. Summer on the fells is one thing, but winter weather in high mountains is different. The open sea is different. Big rivers in flood are different. They are scary, and I know I have no skills for dealing with them. They are too big, too hard, too cold, too remote, too powerful. Too utterly unknowable. I fear them, but somehow have to deal with such fear, in case; and poetry is my only way to approach the unapproachable.

A few years ago, walking round the Kerry coast in southwest Ireland, I discovered that local fishermen from Portmagee, on Valencia Island, would take visitors out to the Skellig Rocks, when the ocean was not too rough. Amazingly, the next day was cloudless and windless, so with only the boatman, a young doctor and a rock guitarist for company, I set off on the two-hour journey into the Atlantic. We passed close to Little Skellig, a huge Gannet colony seething with screaming birds and their young, and were dropped off on Skellig Michael, on whose 700-foot pinnacle a tiny monastic settlement existed for centuries, until the Reformation; their stone beehive cells are exactly as the monks left them. Here is the poem that emerged from the experience.

To the Shining Rock

Horizons pitch up a glittering ten-foot swell.
The 'Agnes Olibhear' from Portmagee
lifts from its wake of islands, gannets, clouds
and rounds the Skellig's head, into cavernous shade.
Seven hundred hollow, stone-slab steps

climb towards a longed-for self-indulgence
in this shell of silent rock.
Through the low door of a cell
my shadow lies on the slate-flagged floor,
a moth pinned as if asleep

in a stone cocoon.
Walls become roof
as eyes adjust, spiral, up to dry
post-holes for spars, that held
possessions offered only to the sky.

I sense this monk had a mattress
of campion, moss and feathers
from Gannet, Guillemot, Fulmar;
some comfort on these cold, old stones.
The wind shears off above, the wide sea far…

* * *

A shadow shivers to life, and I crawl out,
eyes pressed shut against the needle sun
to avoid the void, the adrenalin-shock
of the one small speck, the 'Agnes Olibhear'
homing past Little Skellig on the flowing tide,

the others and our boatman gone
with workmen who fixed the black sea-walls,
tour guides, photographers, everyone gone.
Their silence freezes. How will it feel, alone,
now that the sun of sleep may never set?

If there were water, I would stop to drink.
There is no spring, the boatman had explained,
only hollowed-out stones
and grooves that flow to cisterns
where monks collected all they'd need of rain.

Alan Peacock

But not right here, on this blank peak
nor on the crags below the cabbage-plots
I cannot reach, in any case. Distract me; I feel weak.
So early to be thirsty and alone.
The rocks are cold. I cannot stop to speak.

Collect damp campion, then; more than I need
for added padding; and with a little patience,
some mint-cake and an apple, I dare say,
and old, imagined water, let go the mind
to attend; perhaps to find. Perhaps to pray?

* * *

The sun is low,
Great Blasket set in gold.
Not to share
the shining rock,
the sea set, night-rise.

Prepare to face
so soon the total black;
not to abjure this place,
but make the most of it,
and still get back.

Rehearse again the curving steps,
return, as blind, to the same small door,
the bed of weeds. The cold floor.
no box of matches, and nothing to burn.
Is it too late now to explore?

Stillness starts to thin the blood.
On slabs that radiate alarm,
feet in rucksack, arms round knees,
I fear again those drawn-out, firelit nights
wheezing with asthma as a child; the likelihood,

untreated, of more bronchial, phlegm-filled
nights between prayer and the deep.
Like this they must have lived and worked,
or simply gasped for breath, wordless poems
Hissed at in a secular sleep;

or stories telling the pain
of the early unexpected dead.
Renewals of fidelity.
The sky's unbreakable bars. The smell of rain.
The thick Atlantic cloud. The burial at sea.

* * *

Walking along the narrow monastery wall
above the drop;
whose are these sea-chilled, reaching hands?
What forthcoming justice
do they beg me to forestall?

An old invisible foetal form rocks
to a distant rhythm. Its arms and hands are
bare, goose-fleshed.
What pendulum, what invisible worm
sets the tempo of this stanza?

Alan Peacock

And now the few come chanting near:
their bowed, dead voices crescendo and fade
beyond the wall which is the only ear,
the oratory sounding out
its plainsong in a drowning, night-long shout.

Did they yearn sometime for home,
for laughter, for drink, a pot of stew,
for some known pale-eyed woman,
for her close, insistent groan?
For a touch, a caress; for something simply new?

* * *

Morning comes, whether you sleep or not.
How long was my mind kept
from the long-haul jets heading north-west,
bound for Americay? Stiff in their seats
they too will wonder soon if they have slept,

coming in six miles high
to Labrador's clean day.
Here, dawn is loud; the swell is huge,
white-tops for smacks to surf down.
Cast a cold Gannet's eye . . .

The splendour stares, coming to pass
like this: the saga-sea is all about us.
And so I say to them, stay near to me;
your seventh heaven may yet be
the whole truth of our sixth-sense, out to grass.

The still, sad music of enormity
has ample power, but now no food or water.
Wish you were here? Yes, here?
If only you were, my daughter, right here with me.
By the rivers of Kerry and Cork, and down to Cape Clear,

by the reedy banks of the Okavango
we would crocodile-watch
in a campion-patch
over the unseen Orinoco,
the great grey-green and dried-up Limpopo.

'Sometimes I feel like a daughterless child . . .'

Wild inside, this face admits distress,
left to its own devices for so long,
ready to go toppling from a rock,
the caress of sea-sound and its space
landing me gently in any other place.

For there is no way out; the water is wide,
and my body dies over the ocean.
Whatever it was that waited here
is part of what we never know to fear,
while the world becomes one with the tide

whose current is toward infinity.
It finds a voice to chide, and I reply
that given a choice, I would huddle under
any deck, bound out to anywhere,
to keep my face out of this wind,
all hope foregone of what I came to find.

Skellig* compelled me to begin an exploration of 'what if...': what if I were left there, alone? What does survival entail, physically, emotionally, spiritually? The climber stuck alone in an Andean crevasse—what was in his mind? I discovered, through 'writing out' this experience however, that it is not simply about self. It has become another metaphor for the anomie that stems from changing, almost collapsing communities-in-landscape, and with their change, my lost sense of belonging. I am drawn back to many landscapes—the Pennines, the Southwest coast, Hebridean islands, African savannah, Greek islands, the foothills of the Himalya, in Kashmir—but am no longer part of any of them. Those I know best are taken over. Yet when I fear abandonment alone on a rock in the Atlantic, being lost in a 'white out' on Black Hill, being unable to breathe at 16,000 ft, at the same time, new words seem to rescue me, by throwing down a rope . . .

---

* In gaelic, Skellig (Sceilg) means a shining rock.

Behold, the Sea Itself

Lawrence Sail

Lawrence Sail has published eight books of poems, most recently *The World Returning* (Bloodaxe Books, 2002) and *Building into Air* (Bloodaxe Books, 1995). He has edited several anthologies, including *First and Always: Poems for Great Ormond Street Children's Hospital* and *The New Exeter Book of Riddles*. He has been chairman of the Arvon Foundation, a judge for the Whitbread Book of the Year and the Eric Gregory Awards, and director of the Cheltenham Festival of Literature. In 2004 he received a Cholmondeley Award.

I'M NOT SURE WHEN this love of the sea began. Perhaps it is a simple consequence of being an islander: perhaps a love of the sea was always imprinted, somehow, in the genes. I could, in retrospect, pick out a number of indirect seamarks, from the owl and the pussycat lucky enough to sail away for all that time, to the exultant cry of Xenophon's men when at last they reached the coast. At school, the sea was well represented in a traditional way in prayers, hymns and poems. The intercession for "they that go down to the sea in ships, and occupy their business in great waters"; that eternal father whose arm binds the restless waves; Tennyson's crossing of the bar; Masefield's dirty British coaster. Closer in, there were my father's paintings of the sea. When I was about eight he gave me his oil painting of the Adriatic island of Korcula. The buildings, closely clustered, just fit onto a flat tray of land in the middle distance, backed by the vague mountains or hills of another land beyond. In the foreground, a clinker rowing boat leaning to one side is drawn up on a quay, suggesting the possibility of crossing the strait between land and island. My father returned to this theme a number of times, often in the guise of boats on a beach, with a distant island sometimes so tentatively delineated that it might have been drifting cloud. In the last picture he painted, the boat has become a large carcass, its black ribs rotting on a bleak shore under a purple sky: and the island has drifted out of sight.

When I was old enough to go to the cinema, there was any number of war films in which the sea played a central part: films in which the likes of Kenneth More and Dirk Bogarde, draped with large binoculars over white polo-necked sweaters, anxiously scanned the horizon for U-boats, or skulked in their submerged submarine, periscope down, while the enemy unleashed depth charges overhead. And sometimes the Pathé News would bring details of topical sea dramas such as the January 1952 foundering in the Atlantic of the American freighter *Flying Enterprise* and the heroism of her skipper, Captain Kurt Carlsen, who insisted on staying aboard while the salvage tug *Turmoil* tried to tow her to Falmouth. Such documentary excitement was more than matched by films such as *The Crimson Pirate*, which came out in 1952 and had Burt Lancaster leaping tirelessly, sword in hand, from ratlines to gundeck.

Books too, of course. From a wonderfully illustrated picture book by Bettina, about a donkey called Cocolo who lived on a Mediterranean island, to *Treasure Island*, to Captain Hook, to the Hornblower books, to anything about pirates which I and my mother could lay hands on in Exeter's library. And, close to the top of the list, *The Riddle of the Sands*, the Erskine Childers novel which has one of the best evocations of the sea's unyielding moodiness.

Later, there was the delight of discovering the sea in music: Elgar's 'Sea Pictures', Debussy's symphonic sketches 'La Mer' and, most of all, Vaughan Williams's triumphant settings, in 'A Sea Symphony', of Whitman's celebration of the sea, with the huge, unforgettable exhilaration of the opening chords and words: "Behold, the sea itself". And, in a different idiom, has anyone captured the sea in its summer indolence more pleasingly than Charles Trenet?

For me, all these elements played to the growing allure of the sea, which lay tantalisingly close, only a few miles away from Exeter, where I was brought up. I recall feeling as a boy the unbearable frustration of being close to the water, but not on it. Appalling displays of petulance, no doubt, and the scuffing of shoes on deliberately kicked quayside furniture. But there were also excursions to Exmouth, which often included a trip round the bay, starting from a bouncy plank with wheels on the main beach. The far point was a melancholy clanging bell-buoy. Then, when I was eleven, I went to a sailing school at Salcombe. We learnt in fourteen-footers, clinker-built and gaff-rigged. Pure magic, and not only the sailing but, for instance, rowing a tiny pram round the lower part of the estuary alone at night, whirlpools of phosphorescence twisting away and down at each pull on the oars. Later, we were allowed to venture seaward from the harbour clinker, past the Wolf Rock and over the bar and out into the first heave of the broad slow swell. Later still, there was a voyage in a fifteen foot sailing dinghy, an Albacore, across the channel and up past Belgium to the Dutch islands.

English has had its share of poets who have trawled the ocean for image or emblem—think of Shakespeare's use of the sea and nautical imagery, or Milton's depiction of the generating waters in Book 7 of *Paradise Lost*. Among many others, as well as Tennyson, Whitman and Masefield, are Crabbe, Swinburne, Arnold ("The unplumb'd, salt, estranging sea"), Hopkins, Hardy, Yeats ("That dolphin-torn, that gong-tormented sea."), Vernon Watkins, W. S. Graham, Elizabeth Bishop and Derek Walcott. Walcott's 'A Sea-Chantey', with its lyrical evocation of "The lithe, ebony hulls / Of strait-stretching schooners", in the Caribbean context of "The litany of islands, / The rosary of archipelagos", makes a wonderful companion piece to Whitman's 'A Song for all Seas, all Ships'. But for writers the challenge of the sea remains, in purely descriptive terms, that of capturing what will always resist capture. Perhaps they have a harder time of it than the composers. Protean, never the same twice, even when you look quickly away and back, the sea's shifting totality is virtually beyond verbal encompassing, unless you have the inclusive exuberance of Whitman or the linguistic dazzle of Rimbaud. Emblematic of the variety and restlessness of the imagination, the sea's teeming narratives have no end. The spindrift whipped from the wavetops in a gale, the surface a mill of green marble and wild suds. The sidling infiltration into creeks and drowned rivers. Advance, retreat, overfalls, cross-currents, swash, the slow-turning muscle of the deep ocean. The sea rampant and inroading: the sea grey and crouched low. The sea thunderous and roaring: silent and sunlit in dazzling skeins. The sea in its triple layering: the realms of above, on, beneath the surface. And, sometimes, the impersonality of its moods colonised by the human yearning for evocation and meaning.

I can no more imagine the sea's absence from my writing than I could the impact such an erasure would have on those Devon and Somerset coastal lanes which rise steeply to the reaches of high air. Led forward by the high hedges on either side, the eye focuses naturally on the scale of that openness, yet knows what it betokens. In some way that blank sky conveys the presence of the salt acres beneath it, so that even without a map or local knowledge you would sense that you were close to the edge of the land. For me, there is something in this perception of the sea which cannot simply be explained in terms of offshore breezes, the smack of salt on your lips, or the tangy whiff mixed by the tides.

Two of my collections have marine titles—*The Drowned River* and *Aquamarine*, the latter a group of ten sea poems: many other poems are informed by my abiding interest in the theme. I return to it often from the perspectives of someone who never feels better than when on the sea in a sailing boat. These perspectives alter everything, not least the view of the land as it appears from the sea's plunging deck. In estuaries, negotiations between shore and sea produce their own memorable images— a wood running right down to the water's edge, where salt has trimmed the lowest branches level, leaving a fine secret zone of dark shadow above the surface; or further upstream, glistening flanks of sleech exposed by the ebbing tide. On the open sea, the possibilities for delight are equally varied—the exhilarating rhythms of the boat's hull lifting and falling; the steady power of the wind as it lays the lee side into the waves, testing the halyards; the oddity of rain at sea, water pooling on water; at night, the loom of lights and beacons beneath the horizon, complicit, suggestive of the idea of home; or when riding at anchor, the bare mast nodding beneath moon and stars.

Sleech, the loom of lights, neaps, springs—discovering the vocabulary of the sea is a delight all its own, not least when you learn how it has inveigled its way into general usage as, for example, in doing something 'to the bitter end'. The bitts, or bitt end, was the point at which the anchor chain was fastened to the hull, at its most visible when the chain was paid out to its full scope.

Perhaps, finally, it is the sea's endless ambiguities which prove most intriguing. Evolved from the water, we turn back to it. Its cargo of emblems—white sails, black sails, the dove and the raven—is as timeless as its restless commuting between serenity and storm. Some years ago I moved back to Exeter. If not quite within earshot of the sea (despite the thriving urban gulls), at least I feel that the Exe connects me, like an umbilical, to the sweep of the sea's horizons. For those marooned further inland, try listening to Vaughan Williams's 'A Sea Symphony'. In the third movement, a *scherzo*, he perfectly complements the words of Whitman in summoning the forcefulness of an element as good at buoying up as at drowning:

> *After the sea-ship, after the whistling winds,*
> *After the white-gray sails taut to their spars and ropes,*
> *Below, a myriad, myriad waves hastening, lifting up their necks,*
> *Tending in ceaseless flow toward the track of the ship,*
> *Waves of the ocean bubbling and gurgling, blithely prying,*
> *Waves, undulating waves, liquid, uneven, emulous waves,*
> *Toward that whirling current, laughing and buoyant with curves,*
> *Where the great vessel sailing and tacking displaces the surface,*
> *Larger and smaller waves in the spread of the ocean yearnfully*
>   *flowing,*
> *The wake of the sea-ship after she passes, flashing and frolicsome*
>   *under the sun,*
> *A motley procession with many a fleck of foam and many fragments,*
> *Following the stately and rapid ship, in the wake following.*

Yet the sea is no more immune from depredation than the land. To write of it, in the twenty-first century, without at least an implicit awareness of the environmental and ecological threats which it both suffers and presents, would be a strange blindness. These challenges are still to be met.

Rain At Sea

> *It rings the raddled waves, pocking*
> *The long troughs with icy shot,*
> *Replacing the horizon deftly*
> *With its cold, sea-rain ghosts—*

Of the captain pinned in the tall wheelhouse,
His pinched and bearded face that peers
Onto sheer disasters, the oncoming truth
Of irrefutable, house-high crests;

Of the green cabin-boy, so pale
And pretty, felled by sea fever,
Tipped from under the ensign, in the lee
Of the Horn, the crew on deck, grim-faced;

Of the ship that steers through every weather,
Doubling the Cape of Immoderate Hope,
Wheel lashed, bound for the shores of
Dark Narragonia, Never-Never . . .

The rain, the seething rain that falls
Knows more of soft corruption than any
Churning depth. The sea's decks,
Awash, grow wormy as any wreck.

Babbling o' Green Fields

Jane Gardam

Jane Gardam, who has written for both children and adults, is first and foremost a novelist. Her books have won or been shortlisted for all the major literary awards, including the Whitbread for *The Queen of the Tambourine*. Her latest novel, *Old Filth*, is on the 2005 Orange prize shortlist. Her non-fiction includes a book about the Yorkshire of her childhood in *The Iron Coast*.

I HAVE MADE A GLORIOUS DISCOVERY! I have something in common with Shakespeare! Stephen Greenblatt, in his biography, *Will in the World,* has said that "Shakespeare's roots were deep in the country" and "virtually all his relations were farmers". Same here.

The comparison does rather stop there. My puny roots were put down in West Cumberland, a ruffian place seventy years ago. Shakespeare's great English oak spread its branches over the Forest of Arden three centuries before. My ancestors would not have been able to understand his language. Shakespeare would not have been able to understand the Cumbrian patois, which is still fairly incomprehensible today.

But suppose that when I was five Shakespeare, wandering out of time, had turned up at our farm and leaned over the yard gate and looked out over the midden at the orchard and the Rough Ground and the mild green meadows towards the Solway with the Scottish mountain Criffel standing blue in the distance; he would not have felt an alien. Farms are farms. Weather is weather. There are the same dawns and sunsets, summer twilights, drowsy autumn afternoons. The same stirrings of spring, the same lambing-times, haytimes and harvests, the same ice on the water-troughs in winter.

Even seventy years ago my grandparents' farm was old-fashioned. It stood alone, well off a road ("Never live in a village," said my grandmother, "They know all about you.") We had oil lamps in winter, no piped water, no water-closet, no heating but the huge kitchen fire with branches sticking out three feet into the room, dropping white ash on the pink hearthstone that 'the girl', Molly, scrubbed every morning, and when it was dry, decorated with a chalk pattern of figures-of-eight. (A charm against a chimney sprite?) Outside, and it always seemed more natural to be outside, in all weathers, until it was dark, people were everywhere. Even the poorest farms had hired men—often starving Irishmen hired in Wigton market. Children walked to school and back—my father eight miles a day—and then roamed about in the evening if there was not farm work to do. Ronald Blythe, who has lived over eighty years in the same part of East Anglia, says that village children now are like old Queen Mary: they can't recognise a field of hay. Pass down the street of an evening, he says, and there is a television screen glaring in every house. No children loaf about the hedges looking to steal apples. Well, there aren't many English apples to steal.

Farming is solitary now. One man on a tractor, his ears covered with transistors playing music, has replaced two or three families. In Cumberland the schools closed in haytime, old folk and children working together. My father said that as a boy, coming home with the last load, often by moonlight, was the best exhaustion in life.

I remember the harvests. There would be a crowd of us eating our dinners (for some reason called 'clocks') under a hedge, my mother and grandmother and 'the girl' bringing out cans of tea and pale apple plate-cakes, rather soggy. It was the only time I remember everyone getting on well together. We were a coarse, quarrelsome, cantankerous, sardonic, foul-mouthed lot. (Though I never remember any of the men swearing before a woman.) It was no idyll. No *Midsummer Night's Dream*.

Yet there was a sort of poetry in it. My grandfather was a wild, good-looking man who liked his whiskey and had very dark moods. Molly, the girl, was a femme fatale with clear green eyes. Men hung about the yard gate for her—none of them was Shakespeare—and had to be sent off like dogs. I could never make out what it was they wanted.

Molly stayed fifty years on the farm and, when I was six, how I loved her! I think she quite loved me too. Once she laid a dead rat beside me in the barn when I wasn't looking, but when I screamed she was sorry. I never thought of screaming when she and I went together on a Friday night to the hen-house to kill a hen for Sunday. She taught me how to do it quickly, swirling the head round and round on the dusty barn floor until its neck hung loose, its eyes heavy-lidded and bewildered. Seventy years on, the killing of a hen by children is the centre of my latest novel, *Old Filth*. My hero's ayah had killed cockerels when he was a child in the Malaysian jungle as a sacrifice to ensure the death of an enemy. Yet at the time, when I myself was a child, I had no idea I was in any way upset. I would come chatting back with Molly hand in hand to pluck the hen in the kitchen. Then I'd watch granny cook it and thoroughly enjoy eating it.

In that kitchen stood a kist (Viking word for corn-store) filled with Indian corn to feed to the hens when we were not killing them. The corn was cool and shiny, pale gold like little jewels. I would sink my arms to the shoulders in it. My grandfather rested on the kist every Sunday afternoon after the roast chicken, reading the *Cumberland News* and smoking a black pipe. It was the only rest he ever took, dying at last of old age and hard work like his two cart-horses.

His younger son, my uncle, about this time had got rid of his horses and bought a tractor. His farm was Bromfield Hall four miles away, and much grander than ours at Thornby End. I used to walk to it by myself through the fields at five years old. As there were no telephones, nobody would have known if I hadn't turned up and I seldom told anyone that I was going. I had to pass through the village of Blencogo on the way and once I saw that everyone was out on their doorsteps looking down the lane. A small procession was drawing near; some excited men leading a bull and the bull was up to its neck in thick green slime. One of the men was shouting, "Stuck fast in t'mire. It were well-nigh gone." When I reached Bromfield I told my aunt who said that she'd been expecting it. Her friend Bessie Twentyman who had second sight had told here there'd be a beast in the mire. *The Beast in the Mire* became my first published story.

I was about seventeen when my grandfather died and the farm was sold, and at eighteen I went south to the university. I wasn't unhappy. I was doing what my father had done. He was never a farmer, but a schoolmaster, and we had only been on the farm in his school holidays. My time there was up. I'd always known, I think, lying in Granny's spare-room bed, a great brass thing with gold and green half-tester curtains hung with silk tassels, that I was only a visitor at Thornby End. Though my brother became a farmer, like all our cousins and all their children, I have never wanted to farm. Farming has too much heartbreak in it. Three of the family lost everything in the latest Foot and Mouth, none of them has ever had 'a foreign holiday'. But odder than that, none of them cares for books. Shakespeare gazing over their fields would mean nothing to them.

But there has never been a year when I haven't been back to Cumbria, always with a book to write. Ten years ago I took over from Melvyn Bragg as Patron of a Solway Arts Club at Wheyrigg, which meets in a pub five fields from where the farm once stood. The landscape is much the same, though the lanes are tarmac now and there are fewer yellow-hammers quarrelling in the hedges. Though Windscale is not far away, amazingly, the place feels the same. My grandparents would know it.

I've been so privileged to have such a childhood and lucky too to get away from it. I've travelled the world. I didn't go abroad until I was twenty-one, to Italy, which was the most important journey of my life, because, coming home, I saw England really for the first time, from the train window between Dover and London. This Kent countryside was nothing like Cumberland or Yorkshire. After the black spikes of Tuscany, the trees beside the railway looked fat and soft like clouds. The grass on the banks below the tidy hedges was tangled with the delicate wild flowers Shakespeare knew. I suppose it was then that I realised that there is country in the south, too.

North or south, I could not possibly live anywhere but in England, even in this new and cruel century.

Snow and Rain

Brian Patten

Brian Patten made his name in the sixties with Adrian Henri and Roger McGough as part of the Liverpool poets, and his mix of serious and humorous work make him hard to equal in performance. His collections include *Grinning Jack*, *Storm Damage* and *Armada* for adults, and *Gargling with Jelly* and *Juggling with Gerbils* for children.

IT'S THE BEGINNING OF THE 1950S—*I am five years old and sitting in the back alleyway behind our tiny terrace house in the shadow of the gasworks; I'm surrounded by overflowing rubbish bins and bits of old mattresses. The smell of jasmine from the backyards battles it out with the acrid smell of cat and dog piss, yet I feel perfectly at peace in these surroundings. I'm reading—or rather looking at—a comic, when suddenly a butterfly lands on my shoe.*

It was a small blue butterfly, the kind of powdery pastel blue you see on the walls of houses in the Mediterranean. I shook my foot and carried on with my comic, because small blue butterflies landing on a child's foot was nothing unusual back then. The alleyway teemed with a variety of butterflies, all feeding from the lilac bushes that grew from the crumbling backyard walls, and from the buddleia that had taken root on neighbouring bomb sites. These back alleyways sealed my fate as an urban poet, a poet of the city, yet they were also my first introduction to the natural world. Butterflies, dragonflies, dandelions, lilac bushes, red campion, and the usual array of cats, dogs, pigeons and sparrows, all sought refuge there along with my childhood self. It has taken me fifty years to rediscover the peace I found there, and to begin to write, and really appreciate, poems about the natural world (though truth, the alleyways were just as 'natural' to the inner-city child).

With a few outstanding exceptions I never considered the 20th century to be a century of nature poets. That last century was more a century of internal broodings. We cannot even read a poem as pure and simple as Robert Frost's 'Stopping by Woods on a Snowy Evening' without loading it with our own private agendas. You remember it? It begins,

Whose woods these are I think I know.
His house is in the village, though;
He will not see me stopping here
To watch his woods fill up with snow.

And ends,

> *The woods are lovely, dark, and deep*
> *But I have promises to keep,*
> *And miles to go before I sleep,*
> *And miles to go before I sleep.*

Is 'Stopping by Woods on a Snowy Evening' a nature poem? Or a poem about peace? Or about regretting having to move on? In the end it does not matter. Robert Frost's poem will survive for as long as poetry is read. And that last, magic verse is the reason. What were the promises he was so desperate to keep? What would happen on that many-mile long journey he simply had to undertake? Along with Wilfred Owen, Frost is one of the poets who helped me create my own path. One that led me out of the dark wood that was Byron and Wordsworth, and all the other ancient poets that teachers thought we should be introduced to (because they themselves knew of few others). We were far too young for those poets. Maybe I like the Frost poem so much because it makes me feel peaceful, and because *all* poems about snow remind me of one winter night in my street when I was about eight years old. I sneaked to the window attracted not by noise, but by the absence of noise, and looked out . . .

It was fifty years after the event it describes that I wrote the following:

Remembering Snow

> *I did not sleep last night.*
> *The falling snow was beautiful and white.*
> *I dressed, sneaked down the stairs*
> *And opened wide the door.*
> *I had not seen such snow before.*
> *Our grubby little street had gone;*
> *The world was brand-new, and everywhere*

There was a pureness in the air.
I felt such peace. Watching every flake
I felt more and more awake.
I thought I'd learned all there was to know
About the trillion million different kinds
Of swirling frosty flakes of snow.
But that was not so.
I did not know how vividly it lit
The world with such a peaceful glow.
Upstairs my mother slept.
I could not drag myself away from that sight
To call her down and have her share
The mute miracle of the snow.
It seemed to fall for me alone.
How beautiful the grubby little street had grown!

Is that a 'nature poem'? There is snow in it . . .

If one was given the onerous task of picking one poet in the whole of the 20th century who was a truly great Nature Poet, it would have to be Ted Hughes. My favourite collection of his nature poems published for children in 1975 is called *Season Songs*, but really they are for anyone who cares to read them. I always thought of Hughes as a sombre man. I remember once a large spider walked across a group of illustrations he had scattered over the floor while he was trying to decide which ones to use in a new book he was putting together called *Cave Birds*. Hughes was delighted with this visitation, and decided the spider was a good omen, sent to help him decide which illustrations to use. Hughes' belief in the healing power of poetry and magic was the equivalent of Robert Graves' belief in the Muse.

I mentioned above how I thought Robert Frost's 'Stopping by Woods on a Snowy Evening' is one of the purest and simplest poems of the last century. I doubt very much that when Frost wrote the poem he realised what a great poem he was writing. He might have realised what he had achieved when he'd finished it, but not while writing it. Poets, when they set out to write a poem, very seldom know the outcome in advance. Often it's a feeling they are trying to capture, and, if they are lucky, the right words simply pour down as a gift from Heaven.

* * *

I always feel a sense of isolation when it rains in the city, when the streets are shiny and full of puddles and cars swish past with people cocooned inside them, especially late at night. Then the swishing noise of the cars sounds like a sighing, as if they, too, long to be home. When it rains in the city people retreat, and it seems the rain separates them, pushes them to the edge of things, so that it has the night to itself: a huge, neon-lit emptiness into which to fall.

Rain in the countryside is a different experience. When, particularly in early evening, I'm walking across fields or down beside the Dart and it rains, I feel at peace, as if the rain is linking all living things. Maybe it is because there are more varied creatures in the countryside—human beings, badgers, foxes, owls, and the rest, all sheltering close by; all involved in the same activity, *all sharing the same moment.*

This feeling about rain might come from a time in my childhood when I first began to need to separate myself from the adults who surrounded me in the tiny, claustrophobic house in which I lived.

I remember once, when the adults were screaming at one another in the kitchen, going out into the back yard and standing in the rain to avoid their fights and the sound of their anger. There was a tin bath hanging from a nail on the back-yard wall. I took it down and sheltered beneath it. The drumming sound of rain on the tin bath drowned out their arguments. It was a lovely sound, a clean sound, one that washed all the misery away. I imagined the rain, solid in the clouds miles away, being blown by the wind across the River Mersey, the parks, the railway sidings, and then falling through space to dance on my tin bath and obliterate those stupid voices and their drunken accusations, and their need to blame one another for the pain they felt at their own failures.

There came a point when, regardless of whether or not the adults were arguing in the house, whenever it rained hard I would go outside and shelter under the tin bath. I imagined I was an explorer sheltering in a tent somewhere in a great wilderness. The gurgle of the drains was a torrential river flowing nearby. Dogs barking in the surrounding yards were wolves. The rain seemed to free my imagination, to transport me far away from my troubled world. I felt I was at one with nature. Absurd, isn't it? At one with nature sitting under a tin bath in the middle of a city, in a street still surrounded by the bombed-out rubble of a then recent war.

Now, half a century later, the rain means something different to me. It no longer obliterates the sound of screaming adults. All those I loved and who hurt me are long gone, all under or mingled into the earth on which the rain dances. Now it feeds and nourishes and glitters, and at night when I walk through the garden in the rain there is no tin bath. Just the dark sky above me, and the glorious rain that still washes away all the pettiness in the world.

Walking the Words

Landscape:
Inscape or Escape?

James Crowden

James Crowden, poet, engineer and ethnologist, was born in Somerset and raised on Dartmoor. He has had a lifelong interest in the land and has worked as a shepherd, cider maker and forester, although now he is working full-time as a writer. His latest book is *Waterways*, the story of the rivers and canals of England, Wales and Northern Ireland.

THE LANDSCAPE MEANS DIFFERENT THINGS to different people. As a writer and landscape poet I have always been fascinated by the way that we interpret and exploit the landscape, and indeed how the term 'landscape' itself evolved linguistically and culturally.

The word landscape has an interesting pedigree. For a start it is foreign and has nothing to do with farming. It was first used in England in 1598. The term 'landskip' originated in Holland as a painter's term to differentiate between 'land scapes', portraits and 'sea scapes'. These Dutch artists did far more than just record the landscape around them: they defined it. They not only gave it a name but by looking very closely at nature they were able to reflect what others had passed by. They gave the natural world a status that had not previously been accorded to it. Paintings up till this point had usually been either religious scenes or personal portraits. The notion that countryside should itself be the main subject of a painting was novel. Certain scenes occurred in the medieval Books of Hours, in illuminated manuscripts—for example in the Luttrell Psalter—but these fascinating vignettes were often only details in the margin. It was this radical step by the artists of putting the working landscape centre stage, which gave rise to a new perspective on people and their role in the rural economy. The farmer, peasant and the farm animal became the subject of enormous attention. They were the portraits.

Landscape soon came to mean a view or prospect taken in from a certain point, often a mountain pass or an escarpment, looking down on a landscape or a river scene. 'A piece of country scenery', 1632. 'A distant prospect—a vista', 1698. 'A bird's eye view—a map', 1723. Today it means the whole countryside, lock, stock and barrel.

What is also interesting is the word 'scape' linked to the Old English word *gesceap* that means to create or form, or in old Teutonic *ordain*. These meanings recognise that land could be made or ordained, and in Holland the reclamation of land from the sea and drainage schemes gave these new views an added importance. People could *make* landscape. The word can also be a verb, to landscape. Today of course we have landscape gardening, the political landscape, the moral landscape; we also have the word escape and 'inscape', the latter from the Welsh poet Gerard Manley Hopkins. Landscape is therefore an integral part of our language and culture. And yet it is very personal. It has a meaning way beyond its agricultural value. The English landscape is something that we all feel we own, it is a vehicle for our own fears and joys. We feel that we have a right to articulate our inner feelings about it, in some cases vociferously. It has now become a political entity, maybe it always was. Landscape has more to do with our subconscious than we realise. It is used widely as a metaphor for our collective unconscious and we use it to reiterate our need for survival. It has a symbolic value. It is a national asset, but whose land is it anyway? What was once God's realm and then the King's and then the Baron's is now up for grabs. It's a landscape which is fast becoming on the one hand organic and local, and multinational on the other.

The common ground, the blasted heath and open downland are now rare in southern England. Suburbia rules supreme; its tentacles stealthily invade the wooded glen. At our peril we stand back and let it triumph. Fight suburbia and its dull monotones at every turn. It is the death knell of rural England.

But for an artist, landscape is much more vital, personal and intimate. Landscape is to do with memory and family, upbringing and working within the landscape, hands-on agricultural work. Hard graft in other words. Only when you have lived by the work of your hands for many years can you truly say that you understand the inner workings of the landscape.

I grew up on the western edge of Dartmoor, with its combination of hard grey granite tors, dark mysterious peat bogs, stubborn hardy horned sheep, frisky cattle, fast-flowing salmon rivers, oceans of bracken and gorse studded with isolated and abandoned farmhouses. Dartmoor still holds me firmly in its grasp. That is the landscape that I grew up in, and it is a landscape that I return to time and time again, not just for inspiration and a sense of belonging but for a refuge, an inner and outer balancing of the mind. It is home in the true sense of the word: inscape, yes, but an inscape that I choose to interpret with words. Others choose painting, music, photography or sculpture to express their feelings about the sense and spirit of place. These artistic activities are a kind of personal 'enclosure' that is subjective—but is it an escape?

If you are using landscape as a retreat from the pressures of the modern world then in a sense, yes, it is an escape as well, but it is a creative escape. In my own life I chose to escape from the conventional demands of a 'promising' career in the army. A strange choice at the time, and I am still not quite sure how I managed that one, but there it is. No doubt I would have made a very 'bolshie' soldier if I had stayed in any longer, always questioning things, but I learnt a lot about landscape. As a soldier you view landscape in terms of defence and cover, movement, concealment and vantage points. Your life depends on it. You read the landscape instinctively and view hidden paths in the same way that a wild animal does. Since leaving the army I made a career out of not having a career.

Maybe it is no coincidence that Dartmoor is riddled with soldiers and military exercises, live ammunition, unexploded shells and red flags. And yet the conundrum is that the periodic exclusion of humankind has to a degree helped to preserve what some call a 'wilderness zone'. The bad winter of 1962–63 left a deep impression on me. Princetown was cut off for eight weeks, whole trains got buried in snow drifts and people started muttering about the bad winters of 1947 and 1891. Dartmoor became 'arctic', with temperatures of -20°C. Landscape changed.

The landscape itself has of course been evolving at a dramatic rate over the last ten thousand years. Man the hunter-gatherer and man the farmer have created many different patterns of exploitation. What is good for one is not necessarily good for the other. It is very much a cheek-by-jowl existence in Britain. To me Dartmoor has never been a wilderness. I see in it the work of farmers, enclosures, reeves, clapper bridges, quarries, hut circles, stone circles, stone walls, ancient trackways, leats, old tin mining streams, china clay workings, warrens, a rich tapestry of human activity—remote but spacious, like the human mind.

As a young teenager I would often roam up there alone for days on end. I revelled in hard frosts. When the bogs froze you could go to places easily that were normally out of bounds. You could make fast progress. Once just before Christmas, I was turkey-plucking in the Tamar valley, another favourite haunt of mine, and I had a day off. It was Sunday, and having part of a salami and a good chunk of cheese shoved in my pocket, I set out from the top end of Burrator and walked alone to Ashburton and back in the day. It was the shortest day of the year, and the caravan I was living in had frozen up, so it was good to be on the move.

Landscape meant navigation, and navigation meant survival. Particularly when the mists came down. You have to be able to recognise sheep tracks, even stone walls and small rivers. You become like a tracker, always locking onto landscape, always clocking it from different views, always creating an inner map that you read time and time again: an inner landscape that you can relate to the real paper map that often lies soggy in your hands. The inner compass is precise and set by a lifetime of walking. And so it is with words. We learn to read landscape; we see it and register it long before we learn to talk and read. It is embedded very deeply in our observations and perceptions. It is a vital part of our learning process, landscape imprinted just as deeply as any language pattern or social code.

Later on I learnt to read rocks and mountains as a climber venturing east towards the Himalayas, spending a whole winter locked in a remote Ladakhi Tibetan Buddhist valley called Zangskar. Here landscape was harsh in the extreme, and agriculture some of the highest in the world, with wheat growing

at 12,000 feet and barley at 14,000. It was a yak-herding economy, and in a sense not dissimilar to Dartmoor in winter, only
winter here lasts for six months. Here I viewed the landscape as
an anthropologist. Very quickly I realised that to truly understand what made the culture tick, I had to understand the agricultural economy, farming and the interpretation of the predominantly irrigated landscape. I put anthropology on the
back burner and took to the life of a casual agricultural
labourer, not in Devon but in North Dorset via the Outer
Hebrides and Bristol Docks. In short I became a peasant for
twenty years. I kept sheep. I took up sheep shearing and
forestry, cider making and night lambing on the western
chalky escarpment of Cranborne Chase between Shaftesbury
and Blandford. I realised that the people I was working alongside had a very particular and intimate view of their landscape.
They had learnt their farming before the war, before the tractor
became god. I started making tape recordings of farm workers,
to capture their interpretations of the landscape, but realised
very quickly that, however intimate the recordings were, the
farm workers could not articulate their inner feelings about the
land. They were too close to it—in fact they were in it up to
their necks and had been for generations. I worked alongside
them, and used poetry as a vehicle for documentation. I used
words in a very particular way to record their lifestyle through
the seasons.

One hurdle maker I knew well, Cecil Coombes, died suddenly of a stroke. I had not recorded him, and so I sat down and
wrote a poem about how I remembered him working. It captured the way in which he worked. It was a documentary style
of poetry, as precise as a film script. This is how my first book
*Blood, Earth and Medicine: a year in the life of a casual agricultural
labourer* evolved. Later it was dramatised by Morna Watson,
who specialised in outdoor community landscape theatre. It
was taking this dramatisation back into the landscape that
made such a powerful effect. One shepherdess from Ashmore
said after seeing the performance, "I now know why I led my

life the way I did." High praise indeed. I once got a hurdle maker to read the poem about Cecil, whilst he was making a hurdle. He read the poem, looked me in the eye and said, "That's it!"

When I explained what the performances were about to an Indian lady, she said, "That is precisely what my grandfather did in Bengal." "Who was your grandfather?" I asked. "Tagore" was the answer. I was lost for words.

Since then I have been intimately involved with recording landscape through working lives in Somerset, Dorset, Devon and Cornwall, in particular the Somerset Levels and Moors, Rivers Parrett and Stour, as well as the Cornish tin mining industrial landscape, above and below ground. I have also recorded the traumatising effect of Foot and Mouth.

Landscape is a vital part of my life, and I have a hunch that landscape poetry so beloved by Wordsworth and Coleridge, and written in contradistinction to the industrial landscape of their times, is due for a revival to counteract the industrial farming practices of today. English landscape is predominantly about food production and animal husbandry. And the animals, the livestock? The unsung heroes of the landscape who chomp away at grass morning, noon and dusk? Sheep and cattle are the true heroes of the landscape. And the casual agricultural workers?

> Their ancestors created what you see.
> The earth tamed, ordered, nurtured.
> Pushing up daisies
> They could not even afford
> Stones to mark their graves,
> Only a slight hummock in the evening light.

Landscape is also nature's music, a refuge from the troubled mind, an inspiration, a breath of fresh air, a quality of light that unfolds with all its intriguing and ingenious mechanisms. Landscape at peace with itself has a healing effect.

You look out to look in.
Landscape is a mirror and in it we see ourselves.

Everything is just as it is
Home is where we come to
When we stop.
Searching and striving
These are foreigners then
The password is no word at all.

Look at the stream and you will see the source
Look at the source and you will see the ocean.

Leaving Tracks

Richard Mabey

Richard Mabey is one of the most innovative and respected writers on nature and the countryside. His ground-breaking bestseller *Flora Britannica* won the British Book Awards' Illustrated Book of the Year and the Botanical Society's President's Awards. Other popular books of his include *Food for Free*, *The Unofficial Countryside*, *The Common Ground*, as well as his intensely personal study of the nightingale, *Whistling in the Dark*. His latest book, *Nature Cure*, chronicles his recovery from severe depression through his relationship with nature.

IN A TIME OF SEVERANCE FROM NATURE, walking has become the new rite of communion. Walking will set you right, mend your heart—and your head. Walking will help you find your place. Walking makes bonds with the earth. It is as easy as putting one foot in front of the other. Or is it?

For Dr Johnson and George Borrow, both great wanderers in their time, making contact with the world through walking took on a quite literal meaning. Both were dogged by recurrent bouts of depression, and to keep some kind of link with reality they used to touch objects—trees especially—on their way. For William Hazlitt, solitary walking was an aid to contemplation, especially amongst familiar surroundings. "I can saunter for hours," he wrote, "bending my eye forward, stopping and turning to look back, thinking to strike off into some less trodden path, yet hesitating to quit the one I am on, afraid to snap the brittle threads of memory." Henry Thoreau also relished 'sauntering', and pondered the possible origins of the word in the phrase *sans terre*, "without land or home, which therefore, in the good sense, will mean, having no particular home but equally at home everywhere". He found that he nearly always sauntered towards the south-west, "where the earth seems more unexhausted and richer".

When I first began walking seriously round my home in the Chilterns, I was a ritualistic saunterer, too. My family had an assortment of euphemisms for it. "Just off to stretch the legs" or "just taking an airing"— as if one was a piece of stale washing. Mine was "Just going Up the Top". The Top was my song-line, a circular beat (to the south-west) that could be done in half an hour, but which meandered through a patchwork of woods and green lanes, every scrap of which had profound and totemic meanings for me. When I was a teenager I took this walk three or four times a week, and soon I was following not just my regular route but, like Hazlitt, my own previous footsteps. I would keep to the *right*-hand side of the lane, close to a blackthorn hedge, cut a corner by a vast oak tree, and head for home along the edge of the cornfield rather than on the footpath a few feet below it. Maybe this obsessive tendency was a relic of childhood superstition, like avoiding paving cracks. But I also found something reassuring in keeping to my own tracks, a sense of holding the precarious world of adolescence together.

I took possession of that walk, turned it into an emotional refuge. I used it for earnest perambulating debates with friends—and also, absurdly, as somewhere to hide from them. When I was barred from the company of my first girlfriend, I used to bury messages from her under the oak tree. I revised for exams along it, with a pocketful of record cards onto which I'd condensed all the information I was nervous of forgetting. I was, I think, beating the bounds on these ritual plods, checking out both my internal and external *terroir*.

But like all well-trodden paths, it became a rut. One warm June evening, aged seventeen, I was meandering Up the Top, doing some last-minute physics revision—the Laws of Action and Reaction, or something of that sort. Halfway along the track, inside a narrow wood, I saw a friend's girlfriend walking towards me. She was a dark, intense girl, rumoured to come from a gypsy family and to be living with my friend, something quite awe-inspiring then. I smiled awkwardly, and she stopped, and, pointing to the edge of the wood, said in a beguiling Irish lilt, "Would you be so kind as to pick some of those poppies for me?" Since the flowers in question were no more than five yards away, I was convinced that, for the first time in my life, I was being propositioned. I panicked, groped for the only excuse I could think of—"I'm sorry, I have an exam tomorrow"—and scuttled off along the path, scanning my fistful of cards furiously. I might have preserved a little dignity if the encounter had happened somewhere less emotionally charged. But I felt she was a trespasser as well as a dangerously fast mover. Up the Top I was, ironically, too sure of my ground.

Later, I found favourite walks further afield. Yet staking-out, first-footing, a kind of colonisation in the head, had become a habit. One walk (still further to the south-west) I took whenever the ritual plod round the Top seemed too clogged with stale memories or northern reserve. It passed through a line of riverside water meadows, where I once saw six cuckoos feeding together. Then it crossed a stream, climbed a little and returned along the foot of a beech hanger. The beeches were regularly blown down in storms, and with each new gap there were startling new views of the woodlands beyond. They were cherry woods for the most part, cloaked with white blossom in April, and later ringed by it, when the petals fell and settled round their rims. There was a flamboyant, southerly feel about the people, too. One regular walker did the circuit in climbing boots, carrying a small dog in his arms. Two others I never glimpsed, but their polished champagne glasses were hidden high in the cruck of a streamside oak.

One May here, I saw the actual moment that spring began, and felt for a moment like a witch-doctor whose spell had worked. There had been nearly two days of cool heavy rain and I had driven south to try to get beyond it. I sat on a log by the side of the stream and watched the cloud begin to lift. Small bands of swifts and martins appeared, drifting in from the south. Then—it seemed to happen in the space of a few seconds—the wind veered round to the south-east. It was like an oxygen mask being clamped to the face, so sudden that I looked at my watch for the time. It went down in my diary: "6 May. Spring quickening, 4 p.m. exactly." So the walk developed its own circular logic. Same views, same log every May 6, same clockwise direction. But it was my structure, not the landscape's.

When I moved to Norfolk two years ago, there wasn't a landscape to appropriate in the same way, even if I'd wanted to. The flatness, the treelessness—they give you no cues, no signposts. The arable land has, in one way, already been spoken for. In the wooded Chilterns it was easy to establish your own niche in the intricate tangle of natural growth and human echoes. But here the fieldscape has been flattened out, simplified. The wetlands are hard to pin down in imaginative charts, too, not because they have been drained of meaning, but because they are elusive.

They shape-shift. They're defined not by landmarks, but by flow and nuance. When I walk around the fen at the end of the lane, it is not the same two days running. The paths vanish underwater. The trees collapse, the reed beds are cut. The half-wild Konik horses are browsing in the alder thickets one day, and wading deep amongst the darting teal the next.

How does the absence of a secure berth, where every track is the road less travelled, affect the influence of landscape on writing? What does it do to the historic role of the walk as *text*, as a medium through which landscape becomes literature? It's no longer as easy, perhaps, as putting one word in front of another.

Many writers used walks to provide narrative structure. John Bunyan's gossipy account of his Pilgrim's Progress mirrored his own wanderings about the Bedfordshire fields and the Chiltern heights. John Clare's poems, ramping with immediacy and what Seamus Heaney called "the one-thing-after-another-ness of the world" conjure up his barely controllable excitement as a boy walker, darting from one side of the lane to the other, "jumping time away". One critic reckoned W.H. Hudson's rambling prose "perfectly echoed the long, slow, unhurried tramping of his feet as he roamed through the gentle southern counties each summer" —though, for me, they echo more the alien footfalls of the pryer.

The patron of literary strollers, though, must be William Cowper. After his first mental breakdown in the 1760s, Cowper went to live with friends in Olney. Like many before and after, he tried to keep his melancholy under control by busying himself with domestic routines, especially gardening and walking. "The very stones in the garden-walls are my intimate acquaintances," he wrote in a letter in 1783. His great poem 'The Task' broke graphically with the contemporary taste for structured prospect descriptions. It isn't ordered to any particular design, but offers scenes, observations, reflections exactly as they might be encountered on a walk. Scale and perspective are repeatedly shifting, so that one moment a wild flower is in focus, the next a whole cycle of work in a distant field. In one remarkable passage, he plays games with his own shadow on a wall, "spindling into longitude immense/In spite of gravity and sage remark/That I myself am but a fleeting shade,/Provokes me to smile".

Was Cowper here close to a different view of walking? A glimpse of it not as a ritual of Perambulation, a way of taking possession of the landscape, but as an opportunity for the landscape to take possession of *you*? I'm much taken these days with feral walking. I make no plans, except to begin and end in the same place and follow as few made paths as possible. Instead I tag along on deer-trails, head for trees on the horizon, give in to the slightest instinct to change tracks, and hope I'm being guided by cues below the level of my conscious attention. Of course free-form walking is no such thing, and you're being prompted by the scribblings and murmurings of countless other organisms. But it feels less like colonisation than those obsessive, self-gratifying circuits of my youth.

This winter, as often, I'm finishing a book, and not walking much. I gaze out of the study, grasping at any diversion. Deer sidle through the orchard. A female sparrowhawk has just caused mayhem at the bird feeder. I wonder whether these outside events influence the rhythms of what I'm writing. Should I try to shut them out? Or are they the landscape strolling in on me, beating its own bounds?

Outside the other window our builders, Roy and Lee, are working on the walled garden. They're laying bricks in Flemish Bond, one pair along, one single across. It's as hypnotic as watching the tide come in. Then, right in front of me, a rat is swimming across the pond. It's seen the prostrate pheasant that fell to a syndicate shoot yesterday, and tries, with a few tugs of the tail, to drag it ashore. But it's too heavy, and the rat swims back to the bank, nibbles some waterweed, as sweet as pie, and bounds like a gerbil across to the bird feeder. It's learning to climb up, but doesn't have things all its own way. Already there's a pecking order: jays and mallards see the rat off; blackbirds just jump in the air.

I feel that somewhere between the rat's opportunist grafting and the measured craft of bricklaying is where I should be steering the words. But I need an airing, and take off for a stroll. There is a Latin tag, *solvitur ambulando*, which means, roughly, that you can sort it out by walking. You often can, except that it may not be the problem you think you wanted sorting. I've ended up on a nearby common. The sun is warm, the grass is riotous with moles, and I just drift about, from hillock to tuft. The moles are editing the turf, which is being stetted back by creeping clover roots and the first shoots of plantain and sorrel. I have the distinct sense that the grassland has, so to speak, a plot, with its own fuzzy logic.

Back home, it's dusk. Fox-time. In his poem 'The Thought-Fox', Ted Hughes imagines the animal walking the land just as he stalks the page, and entering "the dark hole in the head". Outside, the pond level is still rising from some mysterious spring. Immense flocks of rooks fly south-west, as they do every twilight. Lifelines seem to be flowing over and under me. Am I part of them or just watching them? And who is writing this anyway?

On my Way to the Loch

John Lister-Kaye

Sir John Lister-Kaye is a naturalist and author who moved to Scotland in 1969 to work with Gavin Maxwell. He bought and renovated the House of Aigas and its estate, and turned it into a successful field studies centre which concentrates on conservation and environmental education, both national and international. His latest book is *Nature's Child*, an appreciation of the workings of nature, written for his daughter.

I MAY NOT GET THERE. That's the way it is with my brief daily walk. Unlike Henry David Thoreau in *Walking* (1862), I start, I have a plan and a destination; I even know what to expect. But as often as not something pops up, an unplanned distraction—a bird, a plant, an insect—barges into my consciousness and takes over. Just what happens to me today is wide open to chance.

Nature has a word for its best thought. Random. "That's where it's at," my old friend and helper, Dick Bethune, would have said, "Random." He would have been right, of course, we know that now—or at least we think we do. Evolution is, after all is said and done, still only a theory, and there are hundreds of millions of people around the world who choose to reject it in favour of Creationism. Not that Dick had much truck with Darwinian or any other theory. He was a man of the country, a man who thought with his hands and gave to every dawning day its honest worth. Nor would his uncluttered brain have wished to comprehend the staggeringly chaotic route we have all travelled from the primeval ooze, every last, utterly random jink and turn of it, to bring me right here to this woodland path, on this day, heading uphill with the loch in mind.

It is only a thought away—a quarter of a mile at most—but the loch is a cheering thought and a satisfying quarter-mile, winding first through wooded pasture and then, where pines and spruces draw tight and dark, gently zigzagging up the bank of the burn, suddenly bursting out at the dam with soft birches and willows circling its eight acres of cloud-filled sky. I have done it often, probably several thousand times across the decades I have lived here, and part of a regular routine. It never dulls. It's the escape I choose from my desk, or when I need to think, or just to stretch my legs and gulp the mountain air in the innocent, happy belief that it is doing me good. It's available and close and familiar in that soft, friendly way one gets to know a place intimately, all its moods and in every season—yes, like a lover really, who, after the first exhilaration of discovery steadies down to be comforting, yet still exciting and fulfilling.

I set out with the happy expectation of visiting an old friend. Long ago the avenue was a driveway for carriages arriving at a grand house. The horse chestnuts and limes evenly spaced on either side are 150 years old now, branches interlocking high above me so that I feel contained, held close, in their power. The gravel that surely crunched beneath shod hooves and steel-rimmed wheels has long been silenced under the eiderdown of leaf litter, subsumed, drawn back into the soil as though it never was. Now it's just a muddy path.

It is high summer—August. The rooks that clotted those fronded heights with their preposterous twiggy nests have all flown now and the trees are quiet of their boisterous, gossiping ways. The tangled, feathery remains of young that didn't make it still lie here among my footprints. Scavengers have done their work well, leaving only the bare beak and skull protruding from a husk of broken feathers and legs. That's how it goes, evolution: a few make it, many don't. These that didn't have done their bit; they've faithfully played out their tragic little roles and ducked out early, unwittingly gifting their nutrients back to the earth. Nothing wasted, nothing lost—recycled. They have surrendered, fallen at the first fence; but whatever random happenstance tossed them aside is now guesswork. The evidence is long gone, like the flesh. Unfit—that's the word, Darwin's stark damnation that tells us these were not the chosen few to carry forth the precious corvid genes that will keep the rook world a-crowing rowdy spring after rowdy spring, Amen.

Was it just bad luck? Were they unfairly gusted out in a sudden squall? Or were they weak, shoved aside by greedier siblings in the nest? Did they hatch as runts with inescapable deficiencies locked into their deepest coding? Did they succumb to disease? There's no way of knowing now. Nature takes no hostages. Natural selection we call it, whatever the cause; it is Chance and Destiny perpetually whirling in a wild, ranting tango—the utterly ruthless, random selection of us all. Every one of us is being tested, all the time, night and day, fair play or foul, pitted against the slings and arrows of outrageous random fortune—our lot. We do our best. Those of us who make it try not to dwell on those who don't. "That's the way of it," old Dick would say with a shake of his canny Scots head, "and there's no much we can do aboot it." All we know is that there they lie, the fledglings, the ragged wrecks of their own grand plans cut short. The also-rans filtered out so that only the lucky, fittest elite pass on to the next round in life's tough old tournament.

Dick was nearly selected out before his time. He was a tail gunner in a Lancaster bomber in World War II, and they got hit, somewhere out over Bremen, in the dark. Many of those brave lads got burned alive before their plane crashed. But Dick's luck was in that day; it didn't catch fire and they made it home with a jagged hole in the tail only a few feet from where he sat trapped in his crippled turret. That was random all right. "Too bloody random," he would probably say if he were here now, with his characteristic "Hmph!" and a shrug of those old shoulders and a sideways smile; but he's gone. Without a murmur of complaint he took sick and failed with a cancer in his eighty-third year. But he *was* one of the fit; after the war he took a bride and passed on his sturdy old Highland genes to two sons and two daughters in whose faces and mannerisms he is with us yet. Every day I see his son, Hugh, who took over his Dad's job when the old man retired. Dick was like this old path, constant, always welcoming, something known and trusted, pleased to see me wherever I bumped into him, raking up leaves or clearing out a drain, mending a fence—menial tasks to some, but to Dick, jobs worth doing so he did them well, very well. He was a perfectionist and a friend and I loved him for both in equal measure.

I flick over a corpse with my toe. A sexton beetle scuttles out from the empty cave of the rook's body. It is brick red and glossy black in a fine symmetry, handsomely designed like a piece of jewellery carefully crafted and thought out. I wonder why this common scavenging beetle needs to be so dashingly smart. Is this really the result of chaos? Is it pure chance that has selected for this level of apparently meaningless elegance? Or is it mimicking something I don't know about? Does red and black mean 'Keep off!' to would-be beetle devourers, does it signal poison perhaps, or a concealed defence? Or could there be something else at work here too? Many times I have stood and shaken my head in awe, wondering whether a grander scheme than just chance is at work in nature. I block the beetle's path with my foot so that I can take a longer look—and I smile.

In the startlingly vivid autobiography of his Russian childhood, *Speak, Memory* (1947), Vladimir Nabokov, the great writer and lepidopterist, smiles too. Mimicry in butterflies and moths "showed an artistic perfection usually associated with man-made things." He, too, ponders determinism: "Consider the imitation of oozing poison by bubblelike macules on a wing or by glossy yellow knobs on a chrysalis: 'Don't eat me—I have already been squashed, sampled and rejected'. Consider the tricks of the acrobatic caterpillar of the Lobster Moth which in infancy looks like bird's dung, but after moulting develops scrabbly appendages and baroque characteristics, allowing the extraordinary fellow to play two parts at once: that of a writhing larva and that of a big ant seemingly harrowing it. When a butterfly has to look like a leaf, not only are all the details of a leaf beautifully rendered but markings resembling grub-bored holes are generously thrown in. Natural Selection, in the Darwinian sense, could not explain the miraculous coincidence of imitative behaviour, nor could one appeal to the theory of 'the struggle for life' when a protective device was carried to a point of mimetic subtlety, exuberance and luxury, far in excess of a predator's power of appreciation. I discovered in nature the non-utilitarian delights that I sought in art. Both were a form of magic, both were a game of intricate enchantment and deception."

I walk on. After the avenue the path turns right across a farm road and between fields of rough pasture. Here, at a little wooden bridge Dick and I built together many years ago, the burn disappears underground, into a sump that once powered a sawmill, the shell of which still stands among the buildings across the field. The stream is now just a babbling brook—a mill lade—running between dressed stone banks and rippling over a cobbled floor. It sprouts male ferns from its crevices and sometimes, very rarely, I have seen a dipper here—another marvel of adaptation—prising caddis fly larvae from their stony, self-secreted tubes on the bottom of the stream. What drove the wren to enter the flood? What tweak of selection made it submerge for its supper when a million bugs throng the surface of the water? Who taught it to duck beneath the stream and stalk the bottom with its grippy little feet, and adjusted the nictitating membranes across its eyes to compensate for the difference between the refractive index of water and that of air? No dipper today, but the grey wagtail is here, flashing his lemon-yellow waistcoat in defiance of his name. He chose to stay on the surface, flicking and darting from stone to stone, perfecting his art, inflicting random predation on anything with wings that flashes past.

In her Pulitzer Prize-winning *Pilgrim at Tinker's Creek* (1974), Annie Dillard lays it on the line. "We don't know what's going on here. If these tremendous events are random combinations of matter run amok, the yield of millions of monkeys at millions of typewriters, then what is it in us, hammered out of those same typewriters, that they ignite? We don't know. Our life is a faint tracing on the surface of mystery, like the idle, curved tunnels of leaf miners on the face of a leaf. We must somehow take a wider view, look at the whole landscape, really see it and describe what's going on here. Then we can at least wail the right question into the swaddling band of darkness, or, if it comes to that, choir the proper praise."

I follow the burn up through the plantation. The needle litter is dry underfoot and the earliest of the autumn-fruiting fungi, pale, lilac-capped, white-stemmed *Russula* toadstools, have thrust their way through the soil carrying with them a coiffeur of ginger needles. Immediately, slugs have attacked them; their silvery trails home in on this randomly surfacing manna of delicate, tender gills; but never—I have observed—is the whole fungus devoured. There seems to be a compromise going on here, some deeper mechanism that turns the slug away leaving sufficient spore-bearing gills for the *Russula* to spread its genes. Even where woodmice and red squirrels have nibbled them the whole cap isn't taken.

I have no answers. These random thoughts have become a way of life, a game I love to play and part of the reason I come here day after day. I glance at my watch. I'm horrified I have sauntered for so long. Thoreau would not approve; he recommended four or five hours walking every day to keep a man sane and well. I can only spare half an hour and it has already gone, lost in the maunderings of an unashamed nature writer who, deep down, would give gold to have been able to spend all my days out here, working with my hands, like Old Dick. I won't make it to the loch today; I must turn for home, for I have other work to do.

Out in the Woods

Rosalind Brady

Rosalind and her partner Simon are known as Barron & Brady, songwriters. They are acclaimed for their fresh, acoustic style, their articulate sensitive songs, and their sheer joy and verve in performance. Nature, landscape and the environment have always influenced their writing. Recently they decided to work more directly in these areas and this is leading them into collaboration with the National Soil Association and Devon Wildlife Trust.

I WAS BROUGHT UP in contradicting landscapes: inner cities and English gardens and wildernesses, each with their own nature. The smell of old apricots rotting on the branch in the deserted orchard farm in the outback; wild cats and Coca-Cola crates in the alley back of the milk bar; tarantulas hanging on my bedroom wall and then later, Sussex; hours spent in the woods near our small village estate; grey Weald clay on my boots and fingers, smell of the oaks, the downy fields. With Richard Mabey's *Food for Free* tucked in our rucksack, my mother and I would make off across the landscape gathering sorrel, fat hen, leaves and flowers. Later, my first oak leaf fag rolled up in brown paper. Five years on Brixton, in London, wild parties, home at dawn—out with the foxes.

I started writing when I was very young, immediately affected by beauty, by wind and rain, as children are. School, ambition, restlessness and disquiet wrenched me from the countryside—it has been more than fifteen years, but I have made it back.

The Greeks call it Artemis: the feeling of sanctity in that place you love, deep in the woods. Find a place where its spirit and yours are in tune, and you will be abundantly creative. You will have reached your homeland.

I had been ill for months and in a lot of physical pain. I returned to the woods when I was too unwell to be anywhere else. I threw myself into the countryside and meditation, and this journey brought me into an entirely new field of writing and singing.

I longed to find a field, to stretch out under the trees, to rest and dream. I had craved this for many years. And when I finally found myself there I had a vision: flocks of skylarks zooming around like they used to. I only learnt this recently but there used to be flocks of skylarks! Flocks! I had rarely seen one in all my walking. Shortly after this major discovery we saw one, my partner and I. She sang so sweetly, so high, my eyes stung trying to catch sight of her, my neck strained upwards to hear. My heart really aches thinking of her now: this intense love. But a few weeks later her weedy field was ploughed over, her nest on the earth destroyed, her voice gone. Where did she go? It is concerns such as these that began to affect my life and work.

"In the empty blue a lark is calling
. . . in her lonely flight."

I am a singer, but before that a writer. I also loved acting when I lived in London—the fun, the escape. But I did not like the words, the lines, the sentences: I wanted to write my own sentences, I wanted to make sense of beauty and of the lack of beauty, of joy and the lack of joy. I find joy in the country, peace and hope. It is a keener, closer joy than the worldly stage. Sometimes I long to return to the stage. Out in the fields writing, singing, there is a loneliness. When I perform I want just to sing like the skylark, and sing of the skylark. Surely if we bond with her we shall want to protect her as we protect our own friends and families and neighbours?

So it was that simple. I spent a lot of time outside and I grew very fond of a particular place in the countryside—Dartington Hall estate. I read Rumi and Kabir and Edward Thomas—that was all I read for a long time. I fell in love with Rumi. When we fall in love, the layers of outward meaning are torn away. One's being melts and merges with the Other—so it is with love of God, Nature, Allah, Great Spirit, the Beloved, call it what you want. "My home was at Cold Mountain from the start/Rambling among the hills, far from trouble." * My Cold Mountain and place of sanctity is a special wood under the leafless ash trees staring up at the white branches in the blue sky. Many ideas have been seeded here under these trees.

---

* By Han-Shan, Zen master, hermit and poet. See *Riprap and Cold Mountain Poems* by Gary Snyder, Five Seasons Press 1965, and *Cold Mountain* translated by Burton Watson, Columbia University Press 1970.

All quotations in italic are from works by Barron & Brady.

The grazing kine, I learnt from them of time
From cold thistle I learnt to cry
The bluebells spoke of splendour,
The celandine
Has steeped within her petals
A heady wine

This year I discovered the books of John Muir, the Scottish naturalist, founder of the environmental movement, explorer, poet and writer, who emigrated to America in 1849. He is revered in the US, and remarkably little known in the UK.

I love his descriptions of bounding down mountainsides at dusk, back towards camp after days spent in Yosemite, California. He lost his sight after an industrial accident and when he could see again all he wanted to do was spend his whole life in the mountains gazing at beauty, taking notes on their ecology, in a sort of spiritual ecstasy. Unfashionably, at the time, he went on to fight to preserve the wild spaces where the forests were being ripped down to fuel growth in the soaring US economy. He sat in the woods with Teddy Roosevelt, convinced him of the importance of protecting the wilderness, and the first US national parks were created. Muir wrote about the feeling of homecoming he found in the mountains and which he wanted everyone to experience. Forced into a more contemplative life than I had ever known before, I sat in the peaceful woods of Devon and began to recover, and as I started to sing and write again I felt restored; I sensed I was returning home. Walking through the landscape, as I did every day, I became fascinated by the interweaving of mankind with the natural world.

We were born *in the world*, as Edward O. Wilson so clearly points out: not on Mars, or on some desert planet. He states that we belong here, where we grew up. Tear us away, orchestrate our reality, and we begin to suffer. Beyond sport and anything else the most popular American pursuit is going to the wilderness areas of the national parks that Muir preserved; Muir believed we need beauty as well as bread.

Searching for wilderness I found none
Until I stumbled through the wind-lorn gate
Into the small wood
Into this laurelled place
I had been waiting, we knew then
For honesty and grace.

Last year I discovered that The Soil Association is encouraging people to come back onto the farms and into the countryside. "Over the last 50 years we have increasingly lost our link with the land and our knowledge of how food is grown," they say. So I visited Bwlchwernen Organic Farm in west Wales, where, in the 1970s, a group of young idealists dreaming and farming the land ploughed new life into The Soil Association. Two of that original group, Patrick Holden (who went on to become Director of The Soil Association) and Nick Rebbeck, still live and work on the same dairy farm.

Nick, who organises and takes school outings to Bwlchwernen showed me the route around the farm on which he takes the visiting schoolchildren. We pause in the snow by some birch scrub he has recently grown on the edge of a field. "This is the secret place I have created for them," Nick tells me. "We crouch here and I say, 'Can you smell that? It is the smell of the musk of a fox.' Wow! they go. We come up this path, but their favourite bit is here."

We approach a broad bank by the meeting of two streams. "This is where we sit and have a barbecue, and the children can play in the stream. We watch the sun go down across the fields beyond the beech trees. They love just playing in the stream."

"Children, even in the countryside," he explains later, "live urban lifestyles." The Soil Association believe that if people connect with the land and the farms, they will start to care not only about the quality of the food they eat but also about the methods and ethics surrounding its production. The seed of Patrick's wish to start an organic farm was itself sown when he was very young, on a trip to a farm. Over the last year we have begun writing songs inspired by the work of The Soil Association, interviewing workers, farmers and food producers and we look forward to participating in The Soil Association's annual conference in 2006. Where else will this work lead? I have a dream of singing in fields and woods and returning songs to the countryside where they used to belong, before they went to the city, to the urban rooms and halls and arts centres. Of course music belongs everywhere, but it also belongs to the countryside. I love to sing in the summertime by some darkly glinting woods near my home. This year we have been invited to sing in the woods of Bedfordshire at a concert to support the replanting of the Forest of Marston Vale.

> *The door to the field lay open*
> *Hope was propping up the lintel*
> *So she planted fruit trees*
> *Blackcurrant, elder and apple.*

Perhaps we could take President Bush and Tony Blair to the Community Forest of Marston Vale to see the urban teenagers' delight in planting trees. Then take them to see the children crouching by the shrubs, entranced by the wildlife, flowers and butterflies on Nick and Patrick's organic farm. Then sit with them on the green desert of a Wiltshire Plain in that deadly silence where no bird sings, no butterfly plays. After these visits, perhaps concern for the environment and the degenerating web of nature would be higher on their agendas. In *The Observer's Book of Wild Flowers* given to me by my mother when I was young (first published in 1937) it reads: "Corn cockle—a common plant. Wandering through our cornfields any time during summer, one is sure to find this beautiful flower" and, "Rock Rose—common throughout the country." These are plants I have never seen wild! They have been stolen from us. To see a field of wild pale flax and pink centaury, as I have just once, is a rare delight. We flock to the countryside on Sundays to see beauty, to wander awkwardly for a while with a vague tugging on the heart of love and loss and recognition. This is the tenderness about which I want to sing.

In the cold wind left behind
The smell of sweet red apple rind

Last year we almost sold up and moved out of Dartington, but when we were on the verge of leaving I suddenly saw the beauty again: the orchards; the smell of crushed apples by the roadside in the cold; the views of the windswept moors; the bony ash boughs in Chacegrove: the silent redwoods on Northwood hill; the watery, ragwort field between the forest side and the river Dart, the Dart! I have seen kingfishers, egrets, a great black angular bird I could not name, heaving out of the river. So I began to write about my particular landscape, her nature and her people.

I feel great excitement walking through the courtyard past medieval Dartington Hall and into the old gardens. The ideas, the innovation, poets, artists, potters, the creativity; it buzzes out of the stones, in the past and in this moment as the College of Arts continues to thrive! Dorothy and Leonard Elmhirst renovated the estate from the 1920s onwards, and they loved the history: the chiselled marks on the archway door where Anglo-Saxon knights had sharpened their arrows; the stamp of the White Hart above the doors, the romance of its dilapidation.

through the archway came the cattle and the crows

I wanted to write a song where past and present collide, because to me the veil between the two at Dartington is very thin indeed. And so I wrote 'Appletown'. That winter, instead of moving, I settled by the wood stove and wrote and talked to older locals in my village and researched their voices, their lives. By the following summer I was also writing about the gardens and about Dorothy Elmhirst, and about John Holland, who built the Hall in the 12th century. I met the Hill family, who for hundreds of years have been tending the orchards around Dartington and Staverton, and in the warmth of their kitchen and their enthusiasm they told me a family story that runs back through time.

Totnes and the Newton Apple
Great Britain, Slap me Girdle
Butterbox are tiny gold
For Gwen's new apple child to hold

Once a few years ago I suddenly saw my past life spread like a river valley behind me—the cut of the silvered river, zigzagging—scooping away. The Dart River valley now surrounds me and zooms off into the distance. The more I dig into the earth here to uncover the stories and voices, the more I find I belong to this place.

There is so much to write. There is the song about the sheep farmer Jack Connabeer whom I interviewed last year. He lived under the wooded hill, Hood Ball—"my mountain," he says—just outside the estate. He was forced out from his sheep farm by changing farm practices—forced in great sadness from his land. There is so much sadness amidst the gratitude (most locals speak of Leonard and Dorothy Elmhirst in very fond terms, and are evidently highly pleased that, as they say, "they put Dartington on the map"): sadness at the noise, the traffic, the loss of working farms, the orchard skills and practices, the inhibitive house prices, loss of the smallness of the village.

She heard softly the clack of the pail
the trains ring of the wheel on the rail
the lowing of cattle and the chant of the boy
all before the noise came

Gone are the days when, as Eddie Guy explained to me, the local children queued at the grocer's shop door at Shinners

Bridge for their Christmas treats; or when boxes of victuals were gifted to every newlywed couple in the village; or in the quiet of a summer evening, every window open, the voice of the mower was heard singing in the meadow. The loss of trust is regretted—doors are locked now—and there are no more village shows and dances in the Hall. The loss of darkness is replaced now with the blare of the sodium lamp. All this is felt and has been expressed to me. I am led to wonder who will really belong to our village when the old folk are gone, if the village is developed to twice its size?

> Who will belong who owns this place when John and Jan have all
>   left us?
> Who will plant the new ones in, graft them on, gather them in?
> Who will bind the orchard root
> And bring the tree to bear a fruit?

I hope I can give back in some small way through my songs a recognition to the locals, past and present, of the work and industry with which they have chiselled the form and mould of this beautiful landscape of Dartington.

But will Dartington ever be my true homeland? No matter how much I dig and dream to find images that bind me here to this village in this landscape, won't I always be restlessly longing for elsewhere? Will I ever return home? But this searching is my work now. I am made to see again and again what really matters—a feeling of belonging to a particular landscape, a feeling of belonging to the natural world.

> The arbour arch under which I pass
> Brief flowers lost among the grass
> They were here before the garden
> They leave us last
> We were beaten by their beauty
> And made to yield our grasp

Setting the Story

Treecreepers, Ammonites and Lost Medieval Villages

Penelope Lively

"In writing fiction I am trying to impose order upon chaos, to give structure and meaning to what is apparently random." Penelope Lively has been a prolific writer of books for children and adults for almost forty years. She has won many prestigious literary prizes including the Booker Prize in 1987 for *Moon Tiger* and the Whitbread Children's Book Award in 1976 for *A Stitch in Time*. Her latest book is *Making it Up*, an alternative biography examining what would have happened in her life if she'd made different choices.

TIME WAS, I used to find getting my hands dirty every day an essential accompaniment to writing: gardening, a bout of digging among the vegetables, some potting up in the greenhouse, a bit of weeding. You thought vaguely about what might go on the page later, while enjoying doing something entirely different. My gardening days are done now, except for some very small-scale stuff, and I miss them. I am a city dweller, because needs must, and I miss also the walks that are another essential escape from life behind the desk.

I still get some walking, several times a year, in west Somerset, which has been the familiar and beloved backdrop to my life since I was twelve. I am passionate about west Somerset; it has no rivals, so far as I am concerned, though I will concede that south Devon is quite pretty, and there is something to be said for the Lake District. Tipping fields, red earth, the long slack contours of Exmoor, the pewter gleam of the Bristol Channel : I have set two novels there, and a non-fiction book, *A House Unlocked*, sprang directly from a house—my grandmother's home—tucked away into that exquisite angle between the Brendons and Exmoor. And now it is turning out to be central to another novel, for some of which I have to reconstruct that landscape as it would have been in the 1930s. Not so very different, in fact; in our particular patch not a single field boundary has changed, and there are barely half a dozen new houses. Well, most of it is within the National Park, thanks be.

I began walking with intent about forty years ago, when I first read W. G. Hoskins' *The Making of the English Landscape*, and my perception of the physical world changed forever. I was living in Oxfordshire then, and homed in upon the regional lost medieval village sites, the drove roads, the hints of prehistoric settlement. I still have my collection of battered Ordnance Survey maps, annotated with scribbled notes. Landscape history has invaded fiction in different ways, for me. A landscape historian is one of the central figures of *The Photograph*, while *Treasures of Time* went archaeological, and Wiltshire-based. But

I suppose that, most of all, the great W. G. Hoskins and his academic colleagues like Maurice Beresford gave me an abiding vision of the way in which the past is indestructible, whether it is the ghosts in the landscape—the undulations of ridge and furrow, the lumps and bumps of a lost village—or the accretions of a person's life. Landscape history became a kind of metaphor.

I have walked Offa's Dyke (or bits of it) and Wenlock Edge, parts of the Cornish coastal path, some of the Roman Wall, and snatches of the South Downs and Brecon Beacons and the Derbyshire hills. No longer, alas, but it is all there still in my head—a marvellous assemblage of some of the choicer places in this prolific land. Everywhere different; everywhere a reflection of what has gone before. For me, walking was never so much a question of mileage, but more a leisurely inspection of all that you came across, from mystifying features of the landscape to wayside plants. These last above all, perhaps. I can still see purple spotted orchids on the South Downs above Ditchling in about 1961, and ramsons in an Exmoor combe, and yellow flag irises in a boggy Orkney field, and the Orkney primrose, which is purple—perversely—and so rare that it grows only there, on one cliff.

A flower book, Petersen's *Guide to the Birds of Europe*, the binoculars— essential equipment. I am an extremely amateur ornithologist, not one of those people who can identify an arctic skua in the pale phase a quarter of a mile away, or distinguish at a glance between virtually identical warblers, but I am intensely bird-conscious, and bird-appreciative. The desk at which I worked for over twenty years looked out over an Oxfordshire garden, and beside it was pinned the Official Garden Bird List. For inclusion, the bird had to have been seen by me from the desk, without standing up or moving to either side. I cannot now remember the total count, but it included Canada Geese and a swan, spotted in flight (well, one does spend a good deal of time gazing out over the typewriter, and it's still work), a parrot escaped from someone's aviary, all the usual garden suspects, and such delicacies as spotted wood-peckers, both greater and lesser, tree creepers, nuthatches, spotted flycatchers and every species of tit on offer. I don't know how I got any books written. Bird-watching is a rarer treat for me these days, but I've learned to find opportunities at the most unlikely moments. Train travel, for instance: the grey wagtails that often patrol station platforms, a statuesque heron glimpsed beside a canal, the white egrets on the mudflats as the train runs beside the Exe estuary. Even Central London has its moments: a skein of geese high above, terns beside London Bridge (I rang up the London Ecology Unit to say: can this be? Yes, indeed, came the reply), the blackbirds and blue tits that valiantly nest in my small cat-infested back garden.

Birds have insinuated themselves into my fiction—alongside gardening, and wild flowers, and landscape history—in the way that any writer's work bears witness to certain abiding concerns. But there is a further concern, which is a stern need for an identifiable physical background to a novel. I need to know where this narrative is taking place, what my characters are seeing around them. So, usually, I put them somewhere that I know, and where I can envisage them. This may simply be somewhere that I have visited briefly: the Crimean coast, which became the setting for a short story; the Blue Mountains of Australia, the prompt for another. My childhood in Egypt, and my powerful memories of Cairo and the countryside beyond amidst which we lived, was crucial to *Moon Tiger*, in which the Libyan campaign of 1942 featured, and to a memoir of that time—*Oleander, Jacaranda*. I may be a reluctant city-dweller, but I do find London of compulsive interest—the loquacity of the place, when you learn how to hear it, the way that it is both now and then, a kaleidoscope of time. Years of wandering around, and looking and reading, came together eventually, in *City of the Mind*, a London novel—one of the hundreds, thousands maybe, that the city must have inspired.

I have always needed to identify things. What is this plant, tree, fossil, insect? My bookshelves are crammed with guides to this and that, and if I investigate some of the titles, I can find pointers to past work. Fossils are an instance: ammonites have crept into at least three books, for which I have needed to be able to cite a particular kind, with the correct Latin name. Hence these manuals about fossils. The scholarly leaflet about woodlice was acquired over twenty years ago, in the service of a collection of stories for children, one of which featured a woodlouse as a central character. But woodlice had had a passing mention some while before, in a novel, and as a result of this attention to the creatures I was proud to find myself mentioned in an article in *Isopoda*, a scientific journal. It was sent to me by the author, who was an oniscologist, which means that his academic subject was the woodlouse, and the article was entitled 'The woodlouse in the cultural consciousness of modern Europe', and was a discussion of the portrayal of woodlice in art and literature. My references were cited alongside that of Flaubert, who has Madame Bovary observe the woodlice on her garden wall and see them as a symbol for provincial sloth and boredom. I was referred to as "the anti-Flaubert of oniscological literature", on account of my more charitable treatment of the woodlouse, and given two paragraphs to Flaubert's one.

Gardens and gardening have played a key role. I always notice indications of garden-consciousness in novelists: Angus Wilson is a prime example. Indeed, if you know absolutely nothing about a writer, I suspect that on the basis of careful textual scrutiny you could build up a pretty accurate picture of their interests, habits, areas of knowledge. Some authors pay great attention to physical background; others leave you in a kind of Sartrean vacuum. Some novels are firmly tethered to a world in which birds sing, the sun rises, weather takes place; in others, the action is all, with the setting left to the reader's imagination. There's a place for both approaches; fiction comes in all shapes and sizes. Nowadays, there are probably fewer takers for the expansive and leisurely nineteenth-century approach to scene-setting. As an adolescent, I read my way through Harrison Ainsworth and Charlotte M. Yonge, with tempered enjoyment of that kind of determinedly indigestible prose, and I do remember sometimes guiltily skipping a page or two of description, in search of some dialogue, or someone actually doing something. Fiction has gone in the opposite direction now, but you have to hand it to the Victorians: they served up the physical world to their readers, down to the last leaf, sparrow and gust of wind.

Above all, there seems to be an abiding relationship between walking and writing. The Lake Poets set the pace, I suppose, literally—Tennyson and others carried on. By the 1920s 'rambling' had become a national pastime, with plenty of writers leading the way—a good healthy escape from an otherwise sedentary way of life, but there's more to it than that. Writing takes place in the head; theoretically, you could write blindfold in a soundproof box. But this solipsism generates an intense need for an alternative, a need for the eyes and ears to take over from the mind, a need to look and listen and wonder what kind of tree that is, and why that field is shaped thus—a need to stop writing, in fact, except that of course in a subliminal way you are not; any or all of it may be grist to the mill, in ways that you could not possibly anticipate.

Landscapes

James Long

James Long was a correspondent for BBC TV News until the end of the 1980s. Since then he has written eleven novels, the most recent being *The Perfect Sinner* under the pseudonym 'Will Davenport'. He lives with his wife Annie in the powerful landscape of a Dartmoor valley, amidst woodland, streams and an iron-age hill-fort.

IN 1993 I KILLED A WOMAN called Claire Merrick. She died near the lighthouse on the Mull of Kintyre, a dangerous road, and although others took the blame, I knew it was my fault. If it had ever come to court, I would have explained that it was unpremeditated, that until I went to the lighthouse I had no thought of killing her. It was the landscape that made me do it. The sight of the steep slope down to the shoreland rocks generated an image of a cartwheeling truck and that was it. Even though it went against the conventions of the genre to kill your heroine in the final pages of the book, it simply had to be done, and poor Claire was soon dead.

After four thrillers I switched to a quieter form of writing, and my landscapes are less blood-stained these days but they still tend to come first. A writer is a gleaner, and those gleanings take many forms: footnotes from history in long-forgotten books, overheard scraps of conversation, something unexpected on the news or the forgotten smell of Mansion House floor polish; but for me, landscapes take pride of place.

Claire Merrick was nearly saved from death. In those days I had some odd relationships with capes and peninsulas. They always seemed such promising places on maps, wrapped around by so much sea, and when inspiration was needed, I was prone to loading the car with any of my children who seemed to have time on their hands and going in search of a promontory. Kintyre looked just right for the ending of this book, but we found ourselves struggling north over the border against a defending storm which beat our tent flat onto our faces that night. In the morning, we shared our dampness with the car seats and crossed to Kintyre on the Caledonian MacBrayne ferry to find that the end of our three hundred mile journey was utterly concealed inside the thickest of fogs. We groped our way to the lighthouse regardless, but we could have been in the middle of Hyde Park for all the good that did. It was only when the mist gathered its skirts for the briefest of moments that we saw the sheer slope down to the rocks, and perhaps it was an unsavoury mixture of frustration and revenge that sent poor Claire to her death.

Well, all right, I've gone straight since then. My heroes and heroines aren't immune from death, but they are likely to meet nicer ends. Landscapes always muscle their way in early. It's as if my characters can't start to walk and breathe properly until they have the right stage on which to strut. I borrow places shamelessly, and quite often I find I can't bring myself to disguise them. There is a village on the borders of Somerset, Dorset and Wiltshire by the name of Penselwood which forced itself into my writing very early on. It is quite unlike any other village I know, spread out in a wandering way around the folded fields. You can find the church easily enough, but then you look around and the village, lacking any sort of centre, has somehow rambled off. Penselwood is packed with the footprints of its history: two Norman castle-sites, a hill-fort, a wood pockmarked with ancient stone-quarrying pits as if it had been the scene of some Great War bombardment. I tried to buy a ruin of a house there many years ago and, when I couldn't, I was forced by the landscape to write a version of its story in the form of a novel called *Ferney*. Whenever my pen ran dry I would take to the A303 and the village would provide for me, bringing me to generous people with the time to tell old stories or showing me another unsuspected pile of stones in a hidden combe. If I just learnt to stand sufficiently still, not something that comes very naturally, I could hear it, smell it and see it properly.

It is the marks the people leave that fascinate and inspire. If I was forced to go back and follow a different path, I would be an archaeologist. We walk on top of the packed sedimentary evidence of our past as the fragments settle to form the latest layer. Before moving to Devon, we lived for many years in Oxfordshire, in another village which I've borrowed for a book. It was an archaeological novel, *Silence and Shadows*, all about what lay under and around the village. I did rename that landscape. Place names were an important part of my story, with their echo of old images. In real life the village is called

Combe, a truly perverse name in that particular landscape because it stands on top of a hill rather than down in the valley below. I called it Wytchlow, from the 'Wycham' prefix which often goes with a Roman settlement set down a side-track from a major Roman road, and 'low' for a pre-Roman burial mound. My attempt to disguise that landscape was thwarted by my American publishers who, quite by chance, designed a jacket with an ancient map as its background. Right in the centre of that map was the village of Combe as if the landscape had objected to my disguise.

A year or two ago, I began to write under a pseudonym and, once again, immediately borrowed a landscape without asking. Another process of obscure historical gleaning had led me to the disputed possibility that Rembrandt came to Hull in the year 1662, so for *The Painter* (by the mysterious 'Will Davenport') I drove in search of a place to root my story and found it straight away in the emptiness of Holderness, the wide expanse of salt-marsh and drained fields along the north bank of the Humber, crossed by dykes and dotted with occasional Dutch-gabled farmhouses.

Sticking up out of that immense time-slip of a landscape was the dark thumb of Paull Holme Tower, the remains of an ancient house, and as soon as I saw it, I knew it was the focal point of the book. Rebuilding a lost house is great fun when you don't need to pay for real builders, and in no time I had restored the tower's twin and set my main characters to the work of constructing a seventeenth-century wing in between them. Once it was up and ready, the landscape and that great bruiser, the Humber, dictated much of the story to me and all I had to do was write it down.

Guilt overcame me when the book came out, and I went back to Paull Holme to track down the tower's owners, to seek their retrospective blessing for my kleptomania. They lived quite some way from it in the most remote part of the wilds of Holderness, down a long, long road to a muddy creek studded with the bones of boats. They were very nice about it, slightly startled and ultimately pleased to find someone else felt the same way that they did about their ancient ruin.

The next landscape to infect me was much closer to home. West of Dartmouth, along the edge of Start Bay lie Slapton Sands, separated from Slapton Ley, the lake behind, by the Line, a narrow ridge of shingle. Inland, across a bridge which was a drawbridge in past centuries, is Slapton village, and in the middle of that intricate and twisted place is another ancient tower, all that remains of the fourteenth-century Slapton chantry. The story of the chantry and the good man who built it is the basis for *The Perfect Sinner*, but as if that astonishing landscape was not enough, it led me to another. A key part of the tale of Sir Guy de Bryan, the chantry builder, is the role he played in the battle of Crecy, and I knew I needed to visit Crecy to understand that more.

If, like me, you were brought up learning your battles and your kings by rote, you may share my misconceptions about Crecy. I was taught about a narrow valley which filled up with a wall of French dead as the English bowmen decimated the advancing army. I was taught how Edward III let the young Black Prince earn his spurs, as the Prince fought desperately on one flank, well away from his father's aid. The landscape told an entirely different story. The valley is a gentle arc the best part of a mile wide. The small English army must have been strung out across it barely two men deep. The windmill where Edward stood and watched was no more than fifty yards from the small escarpment where his son was fighting. Help was always close at hand had it been needed. It was a different story that told itself there. I had a friend with me who had written a Crecy novel years before. He uttered a mild profanity when he saw what it was really like.

That wasn't the end of it. A good landscape always repays a polite visitor. I wanted to know why the king had chosen this rather tricky spot for his defence, and in the middle of the village of Crecy I think I found the answer. It's all in the book.

That blind faith in the scenery's ability to generate a plot has paid off in other surprising ways. Back in my thriller days, I hijacked my middle son and, inspired again by a peninsula on a map, we set off for Quiberon on the Brittany coast. This time the sun was shining, though a ferocious wind was blowing, and when we reached the very tip of that long finger, we saw a sea of white horses beating on the spikes of the outlying rocks. In amongst them were windsurfers, zipping, leaning and leaping. As we watched the wind climbed through force six towards force seven, and gradually the board-sailors called it a day. One by one they came back to safety, muscled youths high on testosterone, until in the end there was just one left, a figure in a red wet suit, far out, taking risks where the others hadn't dared. We watched, along with the rest, for another half-hour until that last adventurer turned for home, wanting to see what sort of hero this was.

She came up the beach, board tucked under her arm, shaking the spray from her long grey hair, the world's most glamorous granny, and five entire chapters of my story typed themselves into my head.

From time to time, I tutor writing courses for the Arvon Foundation and I love to see the way that the special landscape of each of the Arvon centres affects the writing. Totleigh Barton, north of Dartmoor, is a Saxon farmhouse by the banks of the Torridge. Those thick walls breed soft words. Lumb Bank, perched high on the side of a steep Yorkshire valley, looking dizzily down on mill chimneys, sometimes introduces a grittier edge, echoing its former owner, Ted Hughes. From Moniack Mhor, on the Scottish hills, you can see a hundred miles on some days and six feet when the mist comes down. We're still finding out what special influences breathe from the walls of the Hurst, John Osborne's house on the Welsh border.

What next? As I write this, I'm starting to wonder about the private and insular landscape of the Forest of Dean and the marks of its free-miners. I must put that to one side for the time being because I'm deep into the seventeenth-century geography of London, Paris and Long Island, hot on the heels of a great rogue, trying to see it all as it once was. I'm co-writing a book with my oldest son, and I knew for sure he shared those landscape genes when he rang me last week. He had spent the day pacing out the old landmarks of the London of three hundred and fifty years ago, Axe Yard, Seething Lane and Whitehall Palace and from the excitement in his voice I knew London had been talking to him too.

Letting Dartmoor Go

Karen Hayes

After bringing up four children, Karen Hayes had her first novel published thirteen years ago. Since then she has been unstoppable, and has produced novels, poetry, non-fiction and books for teenagers. Place is crucial to her work, and she has set her novels in Brittany, St Ives and Italy. Karen teaches creative writing at the University of Exeter and on Ways With Words holiday courses in Italy.

OUTSIDE MY WINDOW, Dartmoor crouches like a white tiger, covered in icy snow and ready to pounce on people like me who went out today without hat or gloves. My fingers, still thawing, are stiff on the computer keys, my ears still ringing from the wind on the high moorland.

The moor was splendid today. The winter gorse flower, intensely yellow against the snow, seemed to infiltrate the damp air as I tramped along with the dog, and the scent mingled with the odour of sheep, of wet stone, of earth and moss and winter grasses. The skeletal outline of one lone scrub oak stood stark against a fierce blue sky, and at my feet a hidden stream unexpectedly burbled through the undergrowth, clear and clean as the day itself.

Now, as I type, a slow mist is bullying its way over the moor and crowding out every inch of blue. The mist is a strange colour, yellow and blue and purple like a bruise, with streaks of orange as the fading sun makes a last hopeless stab at the sky. I stare out of the window and realise I've been doing this for ages. It's hard to tear myself away from Dartmoor at any time of the year, much more so when I've got a deadline for a novel.

Reluctantly, I turn back to my computer screen. Suddenly the moor is gone and I have travelled through time and space to land in Italy, in the lolloping hills of Umbria. It's spring and oven hot, unseasonably so, and I'm walking down a dirt road past a green field covered with red poppies. They're fierce, those poppies, some crimson, some scarlet, some that seem to shine like burning torches, drawing me into the field, making me want to lie down amongst all that red. But I resist, because I have a meeting with a man I fear and I want to get it over with. He lives over the next hill, still four miles away, not a long distance if it were not for this heat that shimmers on the newly planted vineyards, slinks around the small silver leaves of the olive trees, crawls into my nose, my mouth, my lungs so that I feel I am being suffocated by the heavy hot air.

I loosen the linen shawl around my head, let it drop to my shoulders. I am wearing a long brown overskirt, a loose bodice and my thin worn walking boots. I am a frightened foreigner in these Umbrian hills. Because I am from a city, from Rome, the countryside makes me nervous. The cry of a strange bird unsettles me, as does the air itself, a mixture of hot animal smells, sharp unknown herbs, dry crumbling earth.

I am not me, of course, not now, not the *me* that walked on Dartmoor an hour ago but a young woman of nineteen in sixteenth-century Italy. I have become a character in my own historical novel. And, as I write, the snow-covered moor outside my window disappears without a trace, and the only landscape I know is this sizzling Umbrian one of wooded hills, rolling vineyards, ancient olive groves.

As a novelist, short-story writer and poet who is obsessed with landscape, with place and setting, it is odd that I have never set a book here in my own beloved Devon, where I've lived for over thirty years. Four of my published novels are set in Italy, one in Ireland, one in Cornwall, one in France. The book I am working on now is set in Italy again, but this time, for the first time, I am writing not in the present but in the past, in the Renaissance. But it's still Italy, a country and a landscape that are wholly familiar to me, though not, of course, as familiar as the Devon landscape in which I've lived for most of my adult life.

Once I tried to write a Dartmoor novel. I set it in a village I know well, very close to my own home. The common is a good starting point from which to stride off across the moor with friends, dogs, kids, city visitors—and alone, too. And so here was where I would begin my book. I had a story in my head; I had the timescale (autumn and winter on Dartmoor) and I had my characters. The main one would be Dartmoor itself, which I felt I knew better than I knew any of my other characters. There would be the locals who were born in the village; there would be the incomers too, those who had second homes here or had recently moved. There would, of course, be a clash between them. There was even a Dartmoor spirit, a ghost that haunted the common and the stone circles, for no self-respecting moor village is without its tale of spooks and spectres.

That novel, unfinished, still languishes somewhere in my computer. What went wrong? Today I'm still trying to puzzle it out, but I feel the answer is that I am too close to the landscape I was trying to write about. In this, I believe I am the opposite of many of my fellow writers who feel deeply about the setting of their books. For these, the more attached to the place they are, the more they know it through and through, the better they can write about it.

This is not to say that I am any less attached to my fictional landscapes, nor is my knowledge of them shallow, for I spend weeks, more often months, actually living in a place before I can think of writing about it. Indeed, I try to actually write my first draft in that place, living the landscape, if not the characters, in my books as much as possible. When I wrote my Cornish novel, *Still Life on Sand*, I borrowed a friend's house in St Ives for the months of January and February. The entire book is set there, and it is a story about both the fishermen and the artists who live and work in St Ives today. The characters are all fictional, of course, but I lived in the close community of both for those two months and so the people in my books, their professions at any rate, were quite close to the reality. I knew painters and sculptors who had lived in St Ives nearly all their lives, and they introduced me to others. As for the fishermen, well, their curiosity was soon aroused by my strolling down on my own to the end of Smeaton's Pier every icy winter's evening, staring at the fishing boats rocking tumultuously in the cold black sea, asking numerous questions. I never hid the fact that I was a writer, and soon I had invitations to join fishing expeditions, help in mending the nets, and to eat the fresh sea bass when the catch was good.

St Ives became more than the landscape of my novel; it became focal to the book, a character in its own right. The hours I wasn't at my computer, I was walking around the empty beaches or up around the cliff tops, noting grasses, winter plants and flowers, the colour of the sand at sunrise, the mad thrust and pounding of the sea during stormy weather. I learned to live with the taste and smell of sea salt, and with that extraordinary St Ives light that artists find so impossible to capture. At times, as I walked in this solitary manner for an hour, two hours, I felt as if I were becoming the landscape, that the rocks and seagulls and sand and wind and sea were seeping into my bloodstream. I wrote like a madwoman, finishing the first draft in those two months.

Now, why didn't that happen with my Dartmoor book? When I wrote it, I was as engrossed in the landscape of the moor as I was with that of Cornwall, but somehow the book didn't work. And I think the answer is this: that I looked at the land and the sea and the elements at St Ives with new eyes, fresh eyes, eyes like a child who is daily discovering new wonders in the world. And for me, that approach, those new eyes, seems to be vital as I begin creating a book from a landscape. Dartmoor has been in my blood and bones for too long; I don't feel the zing and tingle of discovery when I walk there, much as I love it and would not live anywhere else. It's a part of me now, and so noting it, observing it, fitting it into a book seems self-indulgent somehow, and also too personal. It would not feel like fiction to me, and fiction is what I write.

Except when I'm writing poetry—and here is when everything I've said just now gets turned around completely. In my poetry collection there are numerous poems in which the Devon landscape—the moors, the hills and valleys, the hedgerows and old stone walls, the narrow winding lanes—all appear, and all inform the poetry. Perhaps this is because poetry goes straight from the heart to the page, while books have to go from the heart through that tunnel we call fiction before they come tumbling out on the computer screen.

Now there is this new landscape in front of me, which I jump into every day after my walk on Dartmoor. Italy again, but this time the Italy of 500 years ago. Already I've had over a month in Rome staying with Roman friends, one of whom looks uncannily like the main character in my novel. No, I didn't steal his appearance for my book, as writers are often accused of doing , for even his friends say that he is the exact replica of the Duke of Urbino as painted by Piero della Francesca. So every evening when I went back to my friends' home off the Campo dei Fiori in Rome, I not only walked past the spot in the old piazza where the executions in my Renaissance novel took place, I also sat opposite the face of a true Renaissance man over spaghetti carbonara and red wine.

During my weeks in Rome I walked the streets, trying to create the landscape of the past in my head from the remains of it still all around me. It was late November, with few tourists around. As I walked, and wrote, the city around me faded until all I saw was Renaissance Rome, built up from the Rome I was looking at now. And when my book moved to the Umbrian countryside, and I moved there too, the same process began. First, becoming re-acquainted with the present landscape, and then letting that slowly vanish as the landscape of the past began to emerge.

And so I'll let Dartmoor go, for now. Not long ago I went to one of the Greek islands, a new one for me, and though it was supposed to be no more than a holiday, I soon found myself scribbling fat pages of notes, writing the landscape of the place in my scruffy notebook while engraving each new hill and horizon in my memory. I bought a dozen books on the island, not tourist books but old yellowing ones I found in obscure bookshops, some luckily even in English. I've not started my own book yet—I'm still in Italy—and I won't until I go back to the island and combine those first impressions with a longer more familiar assimilation. Only then will I begin to write.

But even then, even when I'm on that Greek island in the eighteenth century, I'll still be on Dartmoor in the twenty-first. One is the landscape in which I live; the other where I write my fiction, and I feel lucky indeed to be able to jump back and forth between the two.

Following the Footsteps

Spirit of Place

Valerie Grove

Valerie Grove writes a weekly column in *The Times*. In her biography of Laurie Lee she evoked the greenness of Slad, the clamour of Madrid and the colour of flamenco dancing at Spanish pueblos. She has written Dodie Smith's biography, and at present is working on John Mortimer's life.

I DRIVE OFF with a song in my heart. I am going to the country: heading out on the benighted North Circular Road against the flow of commuters, along the M40 towards the rural fastness in the Thames Valley where, seventy years ago, a barrister named Clifford Mortimer built a weekend cottage. In this house lives his son John, now in his eighties; here he writes his Rumpole books, and here we sit and talk. In the summer we repair to the garden, almost exactly as his blind father left it, but expanded to twenty acres of Oxfordshire: home to rare orchids, magnolias, and wildlife. Although I am an irredeemable townie, born on Tyneside, who has lived in London for the last forty years, I relish these excursions to green and pleasant regions. Writing a biography gives one an excellent excuse to leave town. The life of each of my biographees is ineradicably linked with a particular area—and despite the London links each has had, they have also offered me the chance to get to know the rural places dearest to their hearts.

The first place I enjoyed as a byproduct of writing a biography was the picture-postcard village of Finchingfield in Essex, with its Norman church, hump-backed bridge, duckpond and windmill, as photographed for countless Olde Worlde calendars. Here lived Dodie Smith, author of *The Hundred and One Dalmatians* and *I Capture the Castle*. In fact she was not the rural type. Born in Manchester, removed to central London at fourteen, addicted to the theatre where she made her name with her first play in 1931, she was definitely a girl about town. But while at RADA, in 1917, she had gone home with a fellow student, Barbara Noel, daughter of Conrad Noel, the vicar of pretty Thaxted in Essex. "Never before had I seen so much sky," she wrote. She always remembered the tiny toy-like railway, and the walk across fields and stiles to Thaxted, with its windmill. Fourteen years later, with her third play running in the West End, she and her husband-to-be, Alec, visited the impresario Basil Dean at his country home, Little Easton Manor. The seed was sown. Alec soon found the seventeenth-century thatched cottage known as The Barretts, with three acres of garden, just a mile from the village green at Finchingfield. It was damp and decaying, with broken doors hanging off their hinges. But there were other theatre folk nearby: John Gielgud owned an old mill at Foulslough, and Gwen Ffrancon-Davies lived in a cottage in the next village. Although on her first visit Dodie did not appreciate the cottage's idyllic potential, she later wrote describing the scene. "Five roads led to a green and a pond, surrounded by cottages, and there was an almost indescribable rightness about the composition of the place, just as one finds in great works of art."

With the exception of a fourteen-year exile in the United States, Dodie and Alec remained in Finchingfield for the rest of their lives. After 1955, they went to London less and less, preferring the cottage's comforts—and both died there. Dodie was outlived by Charley, her last devoted Dalmatian, but only for two weeks. Charley was buried by the gardener under the mulberry tree in the garden.

But Dodie's appreciation of East Anglia really centred on the undulating lanes and hidden villages of Suffolk and Essex, so generously endowed with medieval churches, thatched cottages, crumbling castles and manor houses. It was here that she saw, on a never-forgotten twilight in 1934, a Victorian house attached to the ruins of an ancient castle, at Wingfield. This inspired her to conjure up the tale of an impoverished writer living in such a castle, with two daughters yearning for romance. Twenty years passed before she wrote I Capture the Castle, entirely from memory: she was at that time (1945) sitting at a desk overlooking the Pacific Ocean at Malibu, but kept a map of Suffolk by her side. The very names of villages were enough to fill her mind with nostalgic longings, and when she came home she and Alec made a concerted effort to explore, in their pale grey Rolls-Royce, a new village every week, on their shopping expeditions to the half-timbered Tudor market-town of Sudbury. Their companion was their neighbour, Henry Warren, the author of several books on country matters (A Boy in Kent; A Cotswold Year; England is a Village).

In an essay, Warren describes how charmed the threesome were by Suffolk place names: Good Easter, High Easter, Abbess Roding, White Roding, Margaretting, Shellow Bowells, Pharisee Green. They discovered the remote and sparsely-populated Belchamp St Paul, Otten and Walter; and 'the Hennys', villages hidden away in a huddle of hills and dales with narrow, sunken lanes; and the sleepy towns of Lavenham, Clare and Long Melford. On the way they explored isolated manor houses (many later demolished), white weatherboarded watermills, secret gardens and derelict farmhouses, and once, a meadow overgrown with the Great Horsetail.

For me in 1994, the delight was to find that, sixty years after Dodie discovered it, the Essex-Suffolk landscape was essentially unchanged. East Anglia was preserved (partly by unfashionableness) from the depredations of the mid-twentieth century, so any place of antiquity had retained its character. The backdrop to *I Capture the Castle* and the country scenes around Cruella de Vil's Hell Hall in *The Hundred and One Dalmatians* (faithfully drawn by the Graham-Johnstone twins) were recognisable still.

Dodie's village is prey to hordes of coach tours on summer weekends. The village of Slad, in a deep valley near Stroud, Gloucestershire, also attracts its share of pilgrims: not because it is pretty (it is, but not conventionally so) but because it is the scene of *Cider With Rosie*: the village where Laurie Lee spent his boyhood, and returned to in mid-life. The headstone on his grave in the village churchyard reads : "He lies in the valley he loved." And the visitors who used to find Laurie himself sitting outside the Woolpack Inn, still drop in there.

Discovering Gloucestershire (as well as a part of Spain new to me) was the great bonus of writing the life of Laurie Lee. In Essex, Dodie was an incomer. But in Gloucestershire, Laurie was a native. His beloved mother Annie, heroine of *Cider With Rosie*, had brought her four children and four stepchildren from Stroud to Slad in 1917 in pursuit of cheap accommodation after her husband left them: the cottage is still there, along with all the other village buildings and the remains of old woollen mills, on which the valley's prosperity once depended. Slad (originally 'Slade', meaning stream) is in a cleft between steep hillsides, on a road signposted 'Scenic Route' at Birdlip. It's remarkable for its lush greenness, and the loftiness of the beech trees. I came to love waking up there; it always seemed to be sunny. And one weekend I joined a walk led by Jim Fern, a fellow pupil from Laurie's time at the village school, who takes visitors round Laurie's childhood haunts. When I stayed in Laurie's house, and slept in his bed, I would see the view he had every morning, looking south over Swifts Hill, which he loved. He knew exactly where the sun rose and set, behind which tree or hillock, at different times of the year.

Laurie always emphasised that there was nothing wildly romantic or charming about a poor country childhood. "Everybody was poor," he said. "It wasn't all rising fields of poppies and blue skies. A large part of it was lashing rain; chaps walking about in bits of soaking sacking, and children dying of quite ordinary diseases like whooping cough." Yet his most lyrical poems were written here:

> If ever I saw blessing in the air
> I see it now in this still early day
> Where lemon-green the vaporous morning drips
> Wet sunlight on the powder of my eye.

And after spending twenty-five years away from his village—travelling in Spain, living in Sussex and Chelsea—he mustered the courage to return to Slad. Courage, because not all his fellow villagers liked what he had written about them. "Pack o' lies, your book, weren't it?" they would say. But in mid-life he created a rustic idyll for himself, at Rose Cottage and then at Little Court, in the heart of Slad.

Two years before he died, he was at the Stroud Subscription Rooms (town hall) at a public meeting, speaking out against a plan to build ninety houses in the valley, now designated an Area of Outstanding Natural Beauty. The Slad Valley, he declared, was "the green lung that feeds with refreshing air the town of Stroud. If we permit this [development] to go ahead, it will be a self-inflicted wound that not even time will heal.... The valley, with its landscape of tangled woods and sprawling fields, should be left to rabbits, badgers and old codgers like me."

Laurie was a true countryman, who had absorbed the names of wild flowers from his mother (who filled her cottage with them) and local animal lore from the poachers, carters and dry-stone-wallers he met in the pub. With his first girlfriend he had walked to Wotton-under-Edge to see the primroses; he had cycled to Rodmarton Common and picked a rare orchid. His boyhood had been an endless afternoon, spent out of doors with companions, so he knew every blade of grass in every meadow, every stream and coppice and ruined cottage—romantic venues where he later roamed with Lorna, the great love of his life and Muse of his poems. And finally his voice was a low, rustic whisper. Luckily, he recorded his poems and his autobiographical books, so the Gloucestershire timbre of his accent is preserved in perpetuity, evoking the earth and the open air.

And so now to John Mortimer's home territory, Henley-on-Thames and its hinterland in the Thames Valley. "Only some two hours' drive to the west of London," as Mortimer describes it in his novel, *Paradise Postponed*, "but its inhabitants have been spared, no doubt for longer than they deserve, the slow but inexorable march of civilisation . . . Looking down at the landscape spread out below you can see beech woods, thick hedgerows and fields of corn . . ." Though, as he points out, many of the tiled-roofed, brick-and-flint farmhouses have become the homes of pop stars or advertising folk, who have introduced swimming pools, conservatories and saunas.

When Mortimer first came here in 1934 as a boy of ten, the family had a rented cottage at North End. It was a humble dwelling, unchanged since the Victorian era. Next door lived a bodger, a maker of chair legs out of beech trees, and John's playmates in the bracken were the bodger's sons. It seems fantastic, and appalling, that the bodger's cottage was recently on sale for nearly half a million pounds. To own a home here would now be quite beyond the reach of a manual worker or craftsman. Yet there is no outward sign that the neighbourhood has altered. Every time I drive out of Henley, past Stonor Park, and turn off at the sign for Turville Heath, I am struck afresh by the timelessness and peace of the place: the cows dotted on the sloping fields, the narrow lane that winds uphill past farmhouses and woodlands, the lake of mud on the way through the trees that leads to Mortimer's cottage—surrounded, when I first saw it twenty-odd years ago, by bluebells. Every year when the bluebells come out, the Mortimer family takes to the woods for their ritual picnic, harbinger of summer. There are usually four or five horses grazing in the field. It's many years since John Mortimer last rode, and he has never hunted, but he feels so passionately about country pursuits—his wife Penny was a founder of the pressure group Leave Country Sports Alone—he lends his voice to the foxhunting lobby, and joins every march on Westminster, heading the wheelchair division. (If liberty means anything, he declares, it is tolerance of people who do things you don't approve of, like smoking and hunting. Last year he took up smoking purely in defiance of the Labour government.)

The countryside around Henley has been largely protected from development, partly by John's efforts—just as the Slad Valley has by Laurie Lee's intervention. He served for many years as president of BBONT (Berks, Bucks and Oxon Naturalists' Trust) and has lent his name to support Henley's claim to remain a pleasant market town, clinging onto amenities such as the old Regal cinema and the cricket pitch.

John Mortimer found in this region a microcosm of what happened to post-war Britain, which promised such fundamental social change but ended up in the 1980s, with the class mixture as before, at loggerheads: leavened by new characters like the Socialist vicar and the working-class local boy made good as the town's Tory MP. Today, as I drive towards Turville

I often find myself thinking of the 'Rapstone Valley' and 'Hartscombe' and 'Skurfield' and 'Picton Principal', the names John Mortimer uses in the Leslie Titmuss novels, hardly disguising their real identities.

My children have grown up knowing Henley, and the River Thames, and the family-friendly local pubs. But that's because their granny lived here during their childhood years. And we once took a cottage in Suffolk, just a mile from Finchingfield, to sample living in Dodie's environment. But the village where it is easiest to feel a close link with its most famous inhabitant, is undoubtedly Laurie Lee's Slad, because even a stranger can sit in the cosy Woolpack Inn and chat to the locals—and to Laurie's widow, Kathy—who have been coming here for years. Laurie Lee wrote about more than a location, he brought to life a community—and a residue of that old community, I'm happy to say, lingers on.

The Countenance of Nature

Grevel Lindop

Grevel Lindop is a poet, writer and researcher. His work includes several books about Thomas de Quincey, five collections of poetry and *A Literary Guide to the Lake District*. His creative work and his poetry in particular is influenced by his spiritual belief that "it is vital to have contact with the 'deep imagination'—the place where our individual insight and creativity connects with universal archetypes and spiritual dimensions." His current projects include a new book of poetry and a biography, *Charles Williams: The Last Magician*.

AS USUAL, IT WAS KEATS who expressed it perfectly. Travelling with Charles Brown through the Lake District in 1818, he wrote to his brother Tom:

> What astonishes me more than anything is the tone, the colouring, the slate, the stone, the moss, the rock-weed; or, if I may so say, the intellect, the countenance of such places. The space, the magnitude of mountains and lakes are well imagined before one sees them; but this countenance or intellectual tone must surpass every imagination and defy every remembrance. I shall learn poetry here and shall henceforth write more than ever[.]

Keats's sense of the "intellect, the countenance" of the landscape goes beyond what we normally think of as a 'Romantic' response to nature. Grounded in clear seeing—the detail of "slate . . . stone . . . moss . . . rock-weed"—it expresses something both spiritual and visceral: the discovery that this landscape looks back at you.

Keats's words have haunted me for nearly thirty years now: in many places, but especially in the Lake District. Trekking up mountain paths, or scrambling down into rocky gullies near the feet of Scafell; wandering in springtime the winding, deeply-hedged roads between green meadows around Hartbarrow to the south-east of Windermere, I have asked myself—and my surroundings—what that special quality can be. Is it the light, reflected from the unstable, perpetually-moving mirror of the Irish Sea and its clouds? Is it that the geology, the minerals of the area, somehow give a special richness to the vegetation, so that grass is greener, moss and lichen more vigorous, tree trunks more intricately gnarled—especially on rock faces and savagely exposed crags where it seems nothing should be able to grow? Or is it imagination, finding an extra dimension in the details of a place particularly loved and known?

Like other people, writers have always found places saturated with meaning. They need not be country places: Thomas

De Quincey, a middle-aged journalist, used to revisit the pavement outside the Soho house where he had shivered and starved as an adolescent runaway living on the London streets. Norman Nicholson wrote poems about the attic, with its tent-like white ceiling, potted geranium and dormer window, from which, over the roofs of grimy Millom, with its chimneys and steelworks, he could just catch a glimpse of Black Combe. And the attic meant as much to him as the mountain.

But then, we expect the man-made to speak to us. It is the countenance of nature, speaking to us directly, that can really take us by surprise. Yet poetry may often be the catalyst for this. When Keats travelled through the Lakes he was already attuned to the quality of the landscape by Wordsworth's long poem *The Excursion*, which he had read five months earlier. The poem, though much concerned with social and educational matters, is filled with observation on many levels—from the detail of a derelict cottage garden

> *Where two tall hedge-rows of thick alder boughs*
> *Joined in a cold damp nook, [around] a well*
> *Shrouded with willow-flowers and plumy fern*

—to hillsides

> *dappled o'er with shadows flung*
> *From brooding clouds; shadows that lay in spots*
> *Determined and unmoved, with steady beams*
> *Of bright and pleasant sunshine interposed;*

and the "two huge Peaks" of the Langdale Pikes, which "echo back/The thunder's greeting" and also "yield/Music of finer tone; a harmony...of silence" made up of "the clouds,/The mist, the shadows, light of golden suns,/Motions of moonlight" and where "the sun himself,/At the calm close of summer's longest day,/Rests his substantial orb"—for on midsummer day the sun, seen from Little Langdale, does indeed set between the Pikes.

These observations were the fruit of long dialogue with well-loved places. When William Wordsworth and his sister Dorothy first came to live at Dove Cottage, Grasmere in 1799, they were returning to Cumbria for the first time since their family had broken up on their mother's death in 1778. They were not natives of Grasmere. Born thirty miles further north at Cockermouth, they had to make their way into familiarity with the Grasmere landscape; and they did so by walking, working, looking and giving names. Wordsworth wrote poetry, and worked steadily in the cottage garden. Dorothy, besides working in house and garden, talked to the neighbours and listened to their stories—and to the stories of the many travellers and homeless vagrants who passed the cottage. She brought the countryside into the garden, growing local plants and sometimes (in those innocent days before pesticides and population pressure had made conservation an issue) transferring plants from the wild: "went rambling down by the lake side—" she wrote in her journal for 3 June 1800—"got Lockety Goldings [globeflower], strawberries etc., and planted." The following day she "rambled on the hill above the house, gathered wild thyme, and took up roots of wild columbine."

Like her brother, she observed silently and acutely:

Our favourite birch tree . . . was yielding to the gusty wind with all its tender twigs, the sun shone upon it, and it glanced in the sun like a flying sunshiny shower. It was a tree in shape, with stem and branches, but it was like a Spirit of water. The sun went in, and it resumed its purplish appearance . . .

Like any family, they had their own names for certain places—either because they didn't at first know the usual names, or to emphasise the special meaning a spot held for them. A small wood a few hundred yards downhill from their cottage became 'John's Grove', because it was a place where their sea-captain brother John liked to walk and think during his visits to the cottage before his tragic death at sea in 1805. A bend in a small stream, with a waterfall and

> *The foliage of the rocks—the birch,*
> *The yew, the holly, and the bright green thorn,*
> *With hanging islands of resplendent furze*

became 'Emma's Dell', Emma being Wordsworth's poetic nick-name for Dorothy. And the desolately beautiful valley of Easedale was known in the family as 'the Black Quarter': an eerie name no one has quite been able to explain, though the valley, seen across the larger vale of Grasmere from Dove Cottage, often does look dark, both because the morning sun reaches it late and because storms can gather there, caught under the slopes of Helm Crag and Steel Fell. This dialogue with the landscape, a quality of attention, a way of letting emotional intelligence res-onate with perception, is reflected in much of Wordsworth's work and particularly in the 'Poems on the Naming of Places' written in their first year or two at Grasmere.

When I began research for my *Literary Guide to the Lake District* I faced the challenge and excitement of following in the footsteps of the Wordsworths and other writers, often in great detail: identifying the views they had taken in, the paths they had walked, the rocks and sometimes even the individual trees they had contemplated and written about.

In Far Easedale, the most distant reach of that resonant 'Black Quarter' which was such a favourite place of the Wordsworths, I was able to find the 'beautiful rock' which Dorothy noticed on December 6 1800 when they walked there "with all the rocks and the woods and the mountains enclosing us round". There really is one rock more beautiful than the rest, and when you see it it speaks for itself. I never found the "Hollow place in [a] Rock like a Coffin" which Coleridge found in the same valley (to which the Wordsworths introduced him) and where, on 18 June 1801, he "lay and slept. It was quite soft"—recording the fact in his own notebook. I should have liked to lie there too. Perhaps someone else will be luckier.

Coleridge's unidentified discoveries are sometimes as evocative as those we can pinpoint. It was my friend the poet and artist Pete Laver, librarian at Dove Cottage, who pointed out to me a passage in Dorothy's journal that tells how Coleridge, walking with her and her brother on the old path between Grasmere and Rydal, discovered "a bower—the sweetest that was ever seen" which Wordsworth also mentions in a later poem, describing it as a "wild cave, whose jagged brows are fringed/With flaccid threads of ivy". Pete had searched for the "bower" without finding it, but believed it was there somewhere. He detailed his searches in his own notebooks. After Pete's shockingly early death (he succumbed to a heart attack on Scafell aged thirty-six), I recalled those conversations. Now it seemed as if in his search for Coleridge's secret bower he had somehow been hunting, unknowingly, for a gateway to the other world. In an elegy addressed to him, a poem called 'On White Moss', I remembered how we had talked

> . . . of the cave Coleridge found
> below Nab Scar: you planned
> to follow all the hints he left
> in some notebook, trace back his steps
> and reach that fable underneath the ground
>
> no one now will reach. But there you are,
> hunched shoulders, toes kicking the stones,
> your frown
> searching the horizon for the next
> sharpedged distinction or joke . . .

and nowadays I can't take that path without thinking of Pete. Every inch of that rock-strewn, bracken-barbed landscape is full of him. The undiscovered "bower" is something given by the landscape to Coleridge, and by him (and Dorothy) to Pete; then passed on to me: something I can perhaps give others, and also reflect back to the place itself.

Part of the meaning of such places, material or imaginary, is their continuity through time. We need to know that there are things which persist, that are not just part of the fashionable and ephemeral. It's often comforted me, facing some difficult meeting or intractable work-deadline, to know that out there, up in the mountains, a certain tarn or waterfall still exists, seen or unseen, doing its own thing or no-thing, unconcerned with whatever is filling my day with tension—a tension which, seen in that perspective, doesn't need to be there.

I tried to capture this in a poem called 'The Beck' about a tree overhanging a waterfall near the foot of Great Gable—

> *a scarlet-clustered rowan*
> *that fluttered unceasingly, as if outside time,*
> *vibrant and motionless at once in the beating of spray;*
> *and the water foaming as if new-uttered that moment*
> *from the earth's interior. Palms on the lichened rocks*
> *(which were alive too with the presence of water)*
> *I lowered myself into the cleft and drank*
> *from cupped hands . . . I would think, I promised,*
> *of that water reciting itself without pause*
> *here, wherever I might be, however preoccupied,*
> *tired or bored, I would remember this,*
> *rock, rowan and water.*

Water, whose traces are everywhere in the northern land-scape, is anciently associated with poetry. Near the eastern end of that path under Nab Scar is a small rectangular pit, walled with slate and partly grown with ferns, a little way behind the garden of Wordsworth's later home, Rydal Mount. You could walk past the spot without noticing it, but this is the 'Nab Well', the spring that supplied the poet's house with water. His regard for it wasn't only practical. When he feared for a time that he might be forced to move from Rydal Mount, this spring was the thing he expected to miss most, and he wrote a poem praising it as "a dear Friend who meets/A parting moment with her loveliest look", and remembering its reflections:

> How often have I marked a plumy fern
> From the live rock with grace inimitable
> Bending its apex toward a paler self
> Reflected all in perfect lineaments—
> Shadow and substance kissing point to point
> In mutual stillness.

Happily he didn't have to leave. The well itself is still there: if you want to quench your thirst from it you can, and perhaps at the same time drink in some inspiration. We are in nature and nature is in us, and that relationship never feels more intimate then when the same water that shapes the landscape, the same water that sustained a poet of the past, is in your own mouth, refreshing you, whether for words or silence.

Biographical Landscapes

Hunter Davies

Journalist and writer Hunter Davies spends six months of the year in London, and six in Cumbria. He is the author of more than thirty books including novels, biographies, most famously of The Beatles, and several books about football and the Lake District. He publishes his own guide, *The Good Guide to the Lakes*, and is President of the Cumbria Wildlife Trust.

I DON'T LIKE WRITING about landscape. All my long-legged life I have avoided fancy dan stuff. I'm not going to start now.

I don't like reading about landscape either. When I see it creeping up in a book, I think, huh, purple prose rubbish alert, I can skip this. Then I think, has he or she run out of ideas? They should go out and do some proper work, talk to people, do some decent research instead of unloading all this landscape nonsense.

And yet I love landscape. We live half of each year in the Lake District surrounded by stunning fells with three lakes within walking distance: Loweswater, Crummock and Buttermere, three pearls on a string. The whole point of living there is the landscape. But I see love of landscape as a private, personal thing, which can't be conveyed or properly enjoyed in words. I don't even like it in films, considering it self-indulgence. My all-time low at the flicks was having to sit through something called *Paris, Texas*, which was all landscape and buggerall content.

And yet, and yet, I have written many books which revolve around landscape, from Hadrian's Wall to the West Indies, walking along or around those places, trying to convey what they're like. But I always prefer to cover the life rather than the landscape, writing around the people, the activities, the history, letting the scenery seep out rather than be centre stage. Now and again I find the odd descriptive paragraphs crawling in under the bedclothes, as I attempt to catch a view, a hill, a beach, then I think—steady on, if I was reading this, I'd be sneering.

All the same, I find landscape absolutely vital when researching books; not necessarily to write about it, but to experience it, know about it, especially in biographies. I can't get a grip, put them in context, understand them properly, take the long view, until I have the person's personal landscape clearly in focus.

I mean landscape in the broader sense: where they have come from, grown up, looked around, been influenced by, written about, sung about, lived in at some time, live in today.

All this is landscape to me, places as well as environment, the landmarks of their life.

I'm thinking back over twelve biographies I have done—yes, that is self-indulgence, something I rarely do. In fact I have never re-read any of my books, apart from looking up odd bits for reference when a reader has written to say, what an eejit, how could you have written that? I am always too obsessed by the present living book to think about the dead ones.

My first biog was of THE BEATLES in 1968. I knew the North-west, the sort of grammar schools they had come from, the council houses two had grown up in, as that had been my own background, but I didn't know Liverpool—never been—so I spent a lot of time up there, wandering around, looking at places where they had hung around, like the Pierhead, Lime Street Station, the Cavern. Seeing John Lennon's house, with its prissy lower-middle-class pretensions, made a lot of things clearer about his attitudes and so called social rebellions.

Hamburg, though, was the biggest eye opener, as it must have been to them, naïve teenagers, thrown into the sleaze, sex and drugs of the Reeperbahn, and by default, thrown together. It was being stuck in Hamburg that made them realise where they had come from. I believed it made them more Liverpoolish, which came out later in their songs. In 1960, would-be pop singers still had to put on a mid-Atlantic accent and sing about New York or California. The Beatles upset that mould, speaking and singing in their own voices, writing about places like Penny Lane which no one outside Liverpool had ever heard of.

I then did a biog of GEORGE STEPHENSON. I had come across his tracks, literally and metaphorically, when doing a walking book across Hadrian's Wall. I saw in the little church at Newburn that he had been married twice, something I had never known. I visited the little cottage in Wylam where he was born. His family of eight had one room, and at eight years old George started work, keeping the cows off the track where the horse-drawn wagons took coal from the pit. I made a vow to come back when I'd completed walking the Wall.

Today, Wylam is a pretty, rural village, desired by Newcastle commuters, but in George's life it was all noise, filth and dust. As I stood there, I thought about these changes in the landscape over the centuries and also about how from this humble beginning, Stephenson went on to change the world in which he had been born. This is often said about famous people, and is usually fantasy or rubbish. In his case, it was true. Until Stephenson, people had moved at the speed of the fastest horse. After Stephenson, our life was never the same again. We now have planes and rockets and space ships, but railways were our first mechanical means of transport. It was this landscape that inspired me to do his biography.

WILLIAM WORDSWORTH came next. His Lakeland landscape was one I already knew quite well, so I didn't need to do too much landscape research, but there were places he loved, such as the Duddon Valley, that I had never visited.

The houses where he lived provide an understanding to much that happened in his life, such as his birthplace in Cockermouth. It is still the handsomest house in Main Street, recently well renovated by the National Trust, with an idyllic garden backing onto the river. His hatred of the Lowther family, the owners of the house, for whom his father worked, and his left-wing views as a young man, stem from the fact that when his father tragically died, the Lowthers never paid over the money the family was owed. This blighted his life for many decades.

Going to Dove Cottage you can see the wallpaper walls where they all crouched in the cold—walls papered with newspapers, in a pathetic attempt to make it warmer.

I never went to France. Can't remember why now, but I always regretted it. I just had so much material. When you do the life of someone who lived to eighty, which is something I hope never to do again, there is too much to get your head round.

In France, at a place called Blois near Orleans, Wordsworth as a young man had an affair with a French girl, Annette

Vallon, who gave birth to his daughter. This was never known about in his lifetime, and would have shocked the nation when he became Poet Laureate and had turned into a high Tory, pillar of Victorian propriety. I should have gone to see the place where it all happened, tried to imagine his affair with Annette *in situ*.

THE GRADES was a biog of the theatrical family. To do it properly, I suppose I should have gone back to Odessa, in the Ukraine, to understand the pogroms their parents had fled from. Instead, I read it up in other books. But I did tramp the East End to look at the schools and buildings where they had lived.

BEATRIX POTTER was another Lakeland subject. I had visited Hill Top, her famous Lakeland home, but I hadn't properly appreciated that she had never actually lived there. Her real home was a few doors away, in another house. She kept Hill Top as a sort of museum. This was an insight into her love of Lakeland traditions, her passion for Herdwick sheep and for preserving all the many farms she went on to buy.

I did attempt a brief bit of landscape setting at the end of the book because I had, by chance, come across her shepherd, Tom Storey, now long dead. I met him in the fields near Hill Top one day and he told me that it was he who had scattered her ashes, in December 1943, three days after she had died, but he had sworn never to reveal the exact place.

In Search of Columbus was about CHRISTOPHER COLUMBUS, published to celebrate in 1992 the 500th anniversary of the 'discovery' of America. I did a huge amount of travelling for that book, most of it self-indulgent— decided I just had to go to Spain, Italy, Portugal and then all over the West Indies. I could not have appreciated what he did, how he sailed all that way, and back, in his primitive little boat, with no map or proper instruments, if I had not been there myself and seen, for example, the myriad of islands he called the Virgin Isles.

I flew in a little plane to the island in the Bahamas, San Salvador, where he first landed, and also visited a remote beach in Venezuela where he first set foot on the continent of

America. But perhaps the most moody place I visited was Porto Santo, a little island off Madeira, where for a time he lived, cut off from civilisation, his dream of sailing across the world apparently shattered. It helped me to describe those years of semi-exile by having been there myself.

I then wrote about ROBERT LOUIS STEVENSON, *Teller of Tales*. Again I used the book as an excuse to travel round the world, following RLS's tracks from Scotland and France to California and Samoa. All these places mattered so much to him, as can be seen from his writings, poems and letters. In Edinburgh, I slept the night in his boyhood home in Heriot Row where he had watched the lamplighter light the lamp outside his house. Still there today, but now electric.

His house in Samoa, which he built with his wife Fanny, has recently been renovated, and you can walk up to the top of the hill where he was buried and see his grave with the famous lines inscribed. 'Home is the sailor, home from the sea, and the hunter home from the hill.' As a little boy, I always used to think the poem referred to me.

With ALFRED WAINWRIGHT, the great Lakeland artist and guide book writer, his life and passions all made sense when I visited the back-to-back terraced house, surrounded by mills, in industrial Blackburn, where he was born and grew up. He died in 1991 and his ashes were scattered on haystacks, above Buttermere, something he had planned for decades. You have to go there, see the situation, feel the beauty, to appreciate his reasons. No, I'm not going to attempt a description, though it's a view I look towards every day I am in Lakeland.

For the life of DWIGHT YORKE, the footballer, I went back to Tobago with him, to meet his mum and family, still living in the same house where he was born, though now they have Georgian-style fancy windows and twice as many rooms. I still find it hard to imagine how he coped with the culture and climate shock, coming to the ice and snow of Birmingham as a young boy of seventeen, knowing nobody, straight from a sleepy, tropical island.

I've also written about GAZZA. Together we produced his autobiography, so I needed to put in his words, as realistically and believably as I could, his love of Gateshead, the parks he played in, the working man's club he used to get drunk in, which meant going there, walking the paths, checking the stains.

With EDDIE STOBART, his origins, like George Stephenson's, were remote and rural, and yet his lorries went on to dominate the nation's transport system. Looking at the map, he would appear to have been born in the wrong part of the country to set up a transport business which passed into national folklore. Cumberland is remote enough, but Hesket Newmarket, his home village, is practically off the map.

With all the books I have done, I like to think they will always be better, richer, if I know the person's personal landscape.

John Clare:
The Poet and the Nest

Ronald Blythe

"He longed to be lost but he couldn't bear not to be found"—his own words sum up Ronald Blythe, critic and writer, who has lived and worked in East Anglia all his life. He has written many books about England's traditions and countryside including *Word From Wormingford* and *Akenfield: Portrait of an English Village*. His latest novel is *The Assassin*.

We can do some writers no greater injustice than to read them primarily for information of their times. John Clare is constantly in danger of such readings. But his inventories were made for his own peace of mind, not our education, although the bird-lists, reminders for him, remind us of the wonderful *Natural History of Helpstone* that never was. When we read his inventories we see a totting-up of what he refused to believe he had lost—and we see everything which, as twenty-first-century country people, we once possessed. For a great many of us are in direct descent from John Clare's landworkers. He leaves little out. He was making his lists at the very moment in agricultural history when there were for the first time more people in the factories than on the farms. He would not have known this. For Clare, field-toil would have gone on and on until kingdom come. The huge changes he witnessed, the coming of the railway, the enclosures, some mechanisation on the surrounding estates, he treated as unwanted disturbances to the old hard way of life which had for him a spiritual quality of such importance that to alter it was a blasphemy. He was for ever counting what it consisted of, right down to the honeydew on the sycamores, to a boy's song, to Mrs Nottingham of the Exeter Arms' description of fifteen will-o'-the-wisps dancing reels on East Well Moor. Nothing was left out, from the footsteps of girls to the shouts of shepherds, from the insect on the stalk to the sound of those same bells which we hear today.

Helpston, Clare's home village, was no Eden—Clare was never clearer than on this point—but it was his. Illness and the powers that be took it from him, or would have done so had he not found a way to take it with him. What is the most repeated, most closely observed, most loved centre of his 'belonging' in his poetry and prose? It is the nest, its secrecy, its intimacy. What is the object of men's ritual discovery and theft? It is the nest. What brought John Clare into stillness and contemplation, into a silence in which he could hear his heart beating? It was the nest with its sitting bird. His finding and watching nests took him through folklore, botany and ornithology into a profound self-recognition. Hence that superb list of nest poems which, whilst giving us such unique observations of nature, give us something extra, the poet in all his strength and song and vulnerability. 'The Fern Owl's Nest', 'The Raven's Nest', 'The Moorhen's Nest', 'The Pewit's Nest', 'The Robin's Nest' and, finest of all, 'The Nightingale's Nest'. These nervous, furtive but complete observations are unique in literature. There is nothing like them.

Birds-nesting was until quite recently a tolerated activity for country boys. Pity, courage—some nests were high—and competition drove it. It was kind to take a single egg whilst the mother bird bravely screamed a foot or two above. The egg was sucked or blown and placed with many others in a cotton-wool drawer, the rarer the better. Seamus Heaney writes of 'boy-deeds' and recalls a particularly daring boy-deed by Michael Collins, a man born to be king or president. As a boy, Collins made a practice of coming down the chute with the hay, whirling from a high loft to the ground in a cloud of dried flowers and grass. Later on, says Heaney, Collins was ambushed in the Pass of Flowers, shot down, having nothing to hold on to.

John Clare was in free-fall all his life. The various and many helping hands held out to save him proved useless. Eventually they caught him and put him in a cage in the asylum. There he went on singing, lyrically, sadly, satirically, nostalgically. None of those who shared his cage gets a mention, only those who continued to live in the freedom of Helpston, many of whom were in the churchyard, or whom he translated to his other native place, Scotland.

Clare's early boy-deeds had to double with child labour, the latter being the custom and the reality. At eight he was wielding a toy-sized flail in the stone barn alongside Parker, his father, though stopping now and then to draw algebraic signs in the killing dust. A pleasant thing happened when he was about ten. Francis Gregory, the young innkeeper next door, got him to run errands and to help plough and reap his eight acres or so of corn. Francis was unmarried and lived with his mother at the Blue Bell.

They were both ill. Looking back, Clare said, "They used me uncommon well as if I was their own." Mother and son lie by the church tower, their helper by the chancel wall. However, continued Clare, "'Tis irksome to a boy to be alone and he is ready in such situations to snatch hold of any trifle to divert his loss of company, and make up for the pleasanter amusements." Birds-nesting in the ordinary way would have topped these amusements, but Clare, in his autobiographical *Sketches*, confesses to a very different pastime. It was that there in Francis Gregory's cornfield he began his 'muttering', his softly speaking aloud of the rhymes which he would later write down in his bedroom, a tile shifted to let in light. He would memorise lines as he walked to and from Maxey Mill, lugging flour. Boys sang, they did not mutter, and eyes would have been upon him, this child talking to himself, a sure sign of something being wrong or different, which is not a good thing to be in a village.

And all this before a Methodist friend loaned him that fragment of James Thomson's poem 'The Seasons'. The other day I found an ancient anthology entitled *Poetry of the Year, 1867* and in it, only three years after Clare's death, scattered among works by Crabbe, Bloomfield, Burns and others were six poems by him. And what lines introduce this collection? None other than those which introduced Clare to poetry: Thomson's

> Come, gentle spring, etherial mildness, come,
> And from the bosom of yon dropping cloud,
> While music wakes around, veiled in a shower
> Of shadowing roses, on our plain descend.

The electric words for Clare would have been 'our plain'. Both Thomson and he were lowlanders, singers of the levels. Something else appeared to have left a memorable mark at this youthful moment, for Clare makes it an important point in the *Sketches*. It concerned his arrangement with the kind Gregorys at the Blue Bell—it was "the only year I lived in hired service of my life". He mentions it because of it being all too close to his mother's plan to put him into domestic service. She had already got him a box for his clothes. He filled it with books. Francis, the farmer-publican, and Clare shared a friend named John Turnill who helped the jobbing boy with his maths. It was Turnill who composed the lines for Gregory's tombstone under the tower.

I thought of John Turnill while exploring Robert Bloomfield's countryside near Thetford. I discovered that the churchyard of his patron Capel Lofft had been recently vandalised for the convenience of the lawnmower, the memorials pulled up and made into paths and a rockery, their tender village verses placed under our feet. Nineteenth-century funerary verse may not be Wordsworth, but it might well be Turnill or some other young man mourning his friend.

Margaret Grainger, in her *The Natural History Prose Writings of John Clare*, sees him always doubling his boy-deeds: his "watching of the night-jar was an inextricable part of his late night wanderings for courting purposes—he had been a lover since he was fourteen—and his searching for ferns accompanied his efforts to throw off ill health." He becomes an expert on cover, learning this essential art—Helpston always had its eye on him—from the birds. "The Mavis thrush", like himself at this moment, "sings like the song of a young bird while learning to sing". Like him, "It loves to frequent . . . old orchards and hedge borders . . . near the village with a song (in December) when it can get shelter and cover as if it loved to treat the village with a song at such a dreary season. (But) as the spring advances its song ceases and it disappears to its more solitary haunts of woods and forests where it builds its nest. Its nest is made of the blades of dead grass moss and cowdung lined with warmer materials of wool and a finer sort of grass . . . The Mavis never forgets her dead ramping grass (*couch grass*) for the outside covering. A plentiful supply of wool within the wool is what birdnesting boys know it by."

In Clare's *Biographys of Birds*, one of my favourite book titles, and in his 'Bird List' which he made for the tantalising *Natural*

History of Helpstone, birds' nests stretch out like an ornithological city. "The Large Wood Owle", by which Clare possibly means the tawny owl, "attacks boys in a bold manner", the Raven builds where it is difficult to climb, the Jackdaw in uninhabited houses; as to Magpies, which sway about in nests filled with teaspoons, well they are apt to keep their loot. It horrifies him to see the overseers of Helpston rewarding boys who kill sparrows and he would give

> *to tyrant boys a fee*
> *To buy the captive sparrows liberty*

as he wrote in his poem 'The Fate of Genius'. The fate of genius in the villages of his day could be quite terrifying. So hide away, hide away. Take cover. Find cover on 'our plain'.

> *Boys thread the woods*
> *To their remotest shades*
> *But in these marshy flats, these stagnant floods,*
> *Security pervades.*
>
> *From year to year*
> *Places untrodden lie*
> *Where man nor boy nor stock ventured near*
> *—Naught gazed on but the sky*
>
> *And fowl that dread*
> *The very breath of man*
> *Hiding in spots that never knew his tread*
> *A wild and timid clan*
>
> *In these thy haunts*
> *I've gleaned habitual love*
> *From the vague world where pride and folly taunts*
> *I muse and look above*

Thy solitudes
The unbounded heaven esteems
And here my heart warms into higher moods
And dignifying dreams

Clare often turns to nests which lie on the ground, and sometimes finds them safest. He himself feels secure in lying low. Fame elevated him and hurt him, and he was sighted by the spoilers. In the sequence of nest poems, among the greatest natural history poems in the language, he finds a metaphor for his happiness and his plight. They are a miracle of close observation, both of himself treading carefully and of a sitting bird such as the pewit brooding "on her unsavoury nest", and of moorhens on their safe "shelved nests". The accuracy of the descriptions result from many lengthy scarcely-daring-to-breathe starings at building material, delicate eggs and parent birds which were not conscious of the poet's presence. These observations reach perfection in 'The Nightingale's Nest', which tells of Clare's nest-finding apprenticeship and, after many boyish attempts at birdwatching, that it needed maturity for him to come close. It is then that he witnesses those connections which touch his own existence.

How curious is the nest no other bird
Uses such loose materials or weaves
Their dwellings in such spots—dead oaken leaves
Are placed without and velvet moss within
And little scraps of grass—and scant and spare
Of what seems scarce materials down and hair
Far from man's haunts she seemeth naught to win
Yet nature is the builder and contrives
Homes for her children's comfort . . .

Clare's nest was robbed of him, shaken to bits and had to be reconstructed in his head. Taken from the nest, he joined those who sang the great songs of exile.

Where It All Started

Where It All Started

Clive Fairweather

Clive Fairweather was a teacher for thirty years. His inspiring teaching of poetry and drama was recognised by the late Ted Hughes, former Poet Laureate. He is one of the West Country's leading traditional storytellers, with a particular interest in mediaeval literature and Victorian social history. He has never owned a car, a television or a computer, and lives in the village of Harbertonford, in south Devon, from where he walks for miles in all directions.

PONDER AND IDENTIFY these words: "The Blesbok are changing ground." Ted Hughes attributed them to Rider Haggard, but in fact they come from John Buchan's novel *Prester John* (1910). They are a coded warning conveyed to David Crawfurd, the hero of the tale. They signal insurrection in a landscape memorably described—majestic, empty and exposed—the High Veld of South Africa. Ted Hughes encountered the quotation in early childhood. His brother had been reading the novel and declaiming the portentous phrase. In a radio broadcast (c1980) Hughes recalled the force with which these words had penetrated "the callow infant sleep of my belated faculties." He claimed that for many years he could re-ignite their first effect simply by repeating the phrase. "Then with one shiver I would experience an explosion of wonderful, joyful energy. I felt there was no limit to where it might take me." This clutch of words jolted a consciousness that would later give a whole fresh construct to the natural world. The ability to see thrushes as "more coiled steel than living" somehow began with the Blesbok [a species of antelope] changing ground.

Similar stirrings are afoot in Buchan's *The Thirty Nine Steps* (1915) or *John Macnab* (1925)—novels that would turn the most within-doors reader into a trespasser, a fugitive, a poacher. Here too, an empty (Scottish) landscape becomes the principal player in the narrative. The "wonderful, joyful energy" it conveys derives its strength and inspiration from the sense of freedom which Buchan associated with his own childhood in Kirkcaldy, Fife, and with two eventful years spent in South Africa immediately after the Boer War. For him, as for many another, service overseas at a formative stage in his life intensified and re-defined iconic images of home. A subsequent urge to revisit and reflect upon these landscapes of the past propelled him into writing.

The same is true of Rider Haggard, twenty years Buchan's senior, who spent six years in South Africa in the 1870s. Haggard was born in 1856 at Bradenham in Norfolk, a true son of the English squirearchy, for whom devotion to the soil, and the reciprocal love and duty between master and man, were as natural upon his own home acres as in the kraals of the Zulus, with whom he felt a great affinity. Haggard's Norfolk diary *A Farmer's Year* (1899) speaks of England as powerfully as does the gesture, famously recorded by Eleanor Farjeon, of the poet Edward Thomas. Soon after Thomas enlisted for war in 1915, he was asked what he was fighting for. His answer was contained within a pinch of earth, which he crumbled between finger and thumb: "Literally, for this."

The landscapes of Edward Thomas' childhood had nothing of the sweep of Buchan's Border hills, Haggard's Norfolk acres, or the South African High Veld. They were the scrubby wastes of Wandsworth Common in the 1880s, relieved by long visits to the railway town of Swindon, where his uncle was a fitter in the locomotive works. His early memories were of throwing stones at rats, moorhens and dead dogs. But beyond Swindon lay Coate Farmhouse, where Richard Jefferies—another farmer's son turned country writer—had spent an intense and solitary childhood. Edward Thomas, who later wrote a biography of Jefferies, had absorbed the older writer's work "in copious draughts". On the final page of Jefferies' most celebrated book *The Amateur Poacher* (1879) he discovered a mantra as powerful as the Blesbok message had been for Hughes. Thomas refers to it as "a gospel and an incantation": "Let us get out of these indoor narrow modern days into the sunlight and the pure wind. A something that the ancients called divine can be found and felt there still."

Buchan or Haggard would have recognised and shared these sentiments, but not perhaps the oceanic yearnings into which they spilled in Jefferies' confessional work *The Story of My Heart* (1883). Here the shadow of illness and isolation darkens Jefferies' celebration of the sunlit air. But solitude and intellectual ferment loitering among the silent fields can always generate strange energies and perspectives. One thinks of Gilbert White (7 October 1790) finding a snake skin in the harvest stubble: "Not only the whole skin but scales from the very eyes are peeled off, and appear in the head of the slough like a pair of spectacles." The wonderful old man describes how he contrived to peer through the lenses of the eyes, in order to see the world as a snake sees it. As a child, Thomas Hardy tried something similar when he lay upon the ground in a sheep pasture, pretending to eat grass, to observe what real sheep would make of this.

When William Langland rigged himself out in shepherd's clothing for a ramble over the Malvern Hills, the fine spring quiet only served to set his mind racing. The result was the teeming, vociferous, political and religious allegory of *Piers Plowman* (c1370–90). The wayfarers who crowd upon his field of vision are viewed as wastrels, thieves and charlatans. Their urge to travel is a moral weakness, giving them licence to boast and tell lies about their journeys for the rest of their days. The literary landscape of the mediaeval world tends either towards marvels or to desolation, whether it be the apples of Sodom, the gold-enamelled singing-birds of Byzantium, or Henry V's remark that war without burning towns is like sausages without mustard. Chaucer spoke from the heart when he wrote:

> *Here is no home, here is but wilderness.*
> *Forth, pilgrim forth! Forth beast, out of thy stall!*
> *Know thy country, look up, thank God of all.*

The landscape to which the mediaeval mind most readily addressed itself was the distant consolation of the Heavenly Jerusalem with its walls of jaspar.

Strange marvels still beguile the view well beyond the 16th century, whether in terms of "moving accidents by flood and field" as chronicled by Richard Hakluyt or Sir Walter Raleigh, or in the labyrinthine landscapes of romance so wonderfully devised by Ariosto, Sidney and Spenser. In the six long artful books of *The Faerie Queene* (1590–96) there is not one realistic glimpse of Elizabethan Ireland, where the work was written—though there is a foretaste of something wisely observed (in

1902) by W. B. Yeats: "Even when I was a boy I could never walk in a wood without feeling that at any moment I might find before me somebody or something I had long looked for without knowing what I looked for." This too is Hughes' magical excitement, differently expressed.

The first serious attempts to locate the individual within the landscape occur in the latter half of the 17th century. The Civil Wars, as John Aubrey so frequently complained, brought a shift in the way that men and women measured their circumstances. A surprising number distanced themselves from conflict by undertaking personal memoirs, diaries or topographical researches. A classical education steered many towards Virgil's *Georgics*, or the poetry which Horace wrote upon his little Sabine farm. This writing was itself the product of civil strife (49–42 BC). To adopt a similarly bucolic outlook was to re-affirm a sanity, permanence and honesty that were associated with the fruitful earth itself. Richard Gough's fascinating *History of Myddle* (1700) illustrates this strategy, though like Gilbert White's quiet exertions at a later date, the work only found its readership in recent times. But country writing finds a voice whenever old and intimate ways of life are threatened with destruction. This remains true whether one considers Virgil and the Roman Civil Wars or the more recent conflict that engendered the soothing melancholy of Watkins-Pitchford's *The Little Grey Men* (1942).

The vigorous emergence of a reading public in the early eighteenth century assisted the uncertain fortunes of Daniel Defoe. His *Robinson Crusoe* (1719) can be seen as the first truly popular attempt to explore one man's relationship with the earth beneath his feet. The book's popularity with the Romantics fed into their concern for 'the child's place in Nature'. The line extends from Rousseau's *Emile* (1762) and Wordsworth's *Prelude* (1805) to Thomas Bewick's *Memoir* (1822), and the comments made by William Cobbett (1822) concerning his own education, gained between the ages of eight and ten, by rolling down a sand-hill in the fields near Farnham, Surrey.

Richard Jefferies' *Bevis* (1882), A. A. Milne's *Winnie the Pooh* (1926), the tales (1930–43) of Arthur Ransome, and many classics of that vintage, offer further opportunities to roll down sand-hills, and demonstrate how eager the leisured classes later became to give their children the freedom of the open air. Ted Hughes' anecdote suggests that such books, even to the inspiration of a single phrase, will become for those that know them, the lens through which the natural world is summoned, studied and evaluated. As Rousseau said of *Robinson Crusoe*, they provide "the best treatise on an education according to nature."

Bewick's *History of Quadrupeds* (1790), another best-seller, offers a different kind of education. For all its diversity and charm, the heart of the work is a commentary upon improved breeds of cattle, sheep and horses. Nature becomes commodity and profit. Defoe and Cobbett, whose careers knew bankruptcy and failure, saw the soil as a matter of economics. Both comment extensively upon bad roads that hinder trade. Appreciation of the countryside means little without ease of access, and funds to pay the tavern bills. On the important route between Conway and Holyhead, the road surface in 1790 was so bad that it was normal to take coaches to pieces and carry them by pack-horse. Wade, Telford, McAdam, Blind Jack Metcalfe were the four great men whose road-building revolution made possible a whole new thrust of landscape writing. It was the discerning eye of the land-surveyor, the leat-digger, the canal builder, the tunnel engineer that helped persuade a wider public to enjoy the picturesque, and generated the wealth to pay for it. In the same way the railway engineers, with their vast cuttings and embankments, stirred the Victorians towards their obsession with geology, minerals and fossils. and gave them a cheap means of transport to pursue their passions.

The excitement of this phase of travel is captured in Turner's painting *Rain, Steam and Speed* (1844). But it burns more clearly and thoughtfully in his *Picturesque Views in England & Wales* (1825–38). Turner's clouds are those seen from the roof of a stage-coach or the deck of a packet-boat, when the traveller knows that he or she is in for a drenching. But the mood is one of adventure and exhilaration. They are the visual counterpart of countless private pleasure trips, such as those recorded so delightfully in John Byng's *Torrington Diaries* (1782–93) or Dr Johnson's *Journey to the Western Islands* (1775). The musical equivalent is Mendelssohn's *Scottish Symphony* (1832), yet another 'explosion of joyful energy'.

Literature's greatest interpreter of spirited journeys, breath-taking scenery, historical antiquities and toiling peasantry, suffused in the patriotic afterglow that followed Napoleon's downfall, is Sir Walter Scott. As the first international best-selling novelist (after Cervantes) in the history of publishing, his hold upon the reading public of his day cannot be overestimated. Yet ever the most modest of men, he attributed his love of old wars, clan feuds, folklore, landscape and history to the hearthside tales and Border ballads he had absorbed in childhood. Collecting the *Minstrelsy of the Scottish Border* (1802) was his first literary enterprise. A scrap of verse from some forgotten singer could always stir his heart. John Buchan, who enjoyed a similar upbringing, tasted the excitement of Scott's *Marmion* (1808) in his own childhood. He wrote a fine biography of Scott in 1932, and with an outdoor adventure story in the best tradition of Scott he caught the imagination of the young Ted Hughes. The circle of literary indebtedness is almost complete.

But ease of travel alters what it touches. The title of Scott's first novel *Waverley* (1814) shrank to the designation of a railway terminus, and soon the mid-Victorians were lamenting what was being lost. Here is Thomas Hughes (1857): "You who are born into these racing railroad times. When there's a Great Exhibition, or some monster sight, every year; why don't you know more of your own birth-places? You all patter French, more or less, and perhaps German; you have seen men and cities, and have your opinions, such as they are, about schools of painting, high art and all that. All I say is, you don't know your own lanes and woods and fields. And as for the country legends, the stories of the old gable-ended farm-houses, the place where the last skirmish was fought in the civil wars, where the parish butts stood, where the last highwayman turned to bay, where the last ghost was laid by the parson, they're gone out of date altogether."

Here, angriest of all, is Ruskin (1849): "The very quietness of nature is gradually withdrawn from us. Along the iron veins that traverse the frame of our country beat and flow the fiery pulses of exertion, hotter and faster every hour. The country is passed over like a green sea by narrow bridges, and we are thrown back in continually closer crowds upon the city gates."

Recoiling from speed and superficiality, Ruskin welcomed the infinitely observed detail which he discovered in the work of the Pre-Raphaelites. The hypnotic realism of the marshy fields at Winchelsea in Millais' painting *The Blind Girl* (1854–6), or the ditch between the willows in *The Hireling Shepherd* by Holman Hunt (1851–2), becomes an invitation to remember England as it must have been. It is the rapt attention that implies farewell. A similar poignancy of focus characterised Kilvert's *Diary* (1870-9), and the scrupulous descriptive accuracy of Gerard Manley Hopkins. Seamus Heaney's Irish ditches are recorded with a Pre-Raphaelite precision which owes much to the verbal edginess of Hopkins.

In the love and understanding of the land shown by all the writers here assembled, and by many others, one influence predominates: this is their individual and personal contact, often in childhood or early in life, with the patient, knowledgeable, unlettered generations that worked the land and never left it. Their ancient and distinctive styles of speech, thought and action, their memories, skills, stories and beliefs became a point of focus for writers like George Sturt, George Ewart Evans, Flora Thompson, Lilias Rider Haggard, George Borrow, Thomas Hardy and Edward Thomas. Higglers and reddlemen, gypsies and ballad-singers, men skilled at stripping oak-bark with a horse's leg-bone, women who could string an eel-bab with a tangle of scarlet wool—they emerge for a legendary moment into the firelight of our reading, and then retire into the dark.

In the march of urban culture, the last of those indigenous country dwellers—those who could read the landscape as a slow, rich and inclusive narrative—are disappearing. Where shall we find such inspiration when they are gone?